"In *Woman of Confidence* Pam Farrel reveals specific steps that lead to courageous faith, purposeful living, and passionate commitment as we live out God's dream for our future. With her characteristic enthusiasm, Bible-based truth, and practical applications, Pam has given us a resource that belongs in the library of every woman who wants to live above criticism and in pursuit of a high and holy calling. Don't miss it!"

—**Carol Kent, President,** Speak Up Speaker Services

"Pam Farrel has a God-sized call in her life that is matched only by her God-sized confidence. This book will help any woman learn to think outside the box and take that big first step toward the adventure and thrill of living the Big Life, the God Life that is waiting inside every woman of confidence."

—**Ellie Kay,** international speaker and author of *Living Rich for Less*

"Pam Farrel is a dynamic, confident, and courageous woman who loves to share God in a way that will lead you to discover who He is and live out the adventure of all He is calling you to. This encouraging resource will empower you to step out and believe God for your part in making a significant difference in a positive way. Get ready for the adventure of your life!"

—**Dr. Catherine Hart Weber,** Hart Institute Director, author of *Secrets of Eve*

"Pam Farrel has written a bo⋯⋯⋯⋯⋯⋯⋯ is a natural cheerleader with a g⋯⋯⋯⋯⋯⋯⋯ve their adventure in life."

—**Jill Savage,** CEO of Hearts at Home and author of *My Heart's at Home* and *I'm Glad I'm a Mom*

"Pam Farrel is the woman's cheerleader of cheerleaders! If you're hesitating about your next step in life or you're under the pile of daily demands, *Woman of Confidence* will reignite your desire to become all you can be. Don't begin a day without knowing how to be a confident woman!"

—**Marcia Ramsland,** international speaker and author of *Simplify Your Life, Simplify Your Time,* and *Simplify Your Space*

"In *Woman of Confidence* Pam Farrel addresses the greatest need of Christian women—lack of confidence and healthy self-esteem. Few women live up to their full potential because they fall for the enemy's lies. They believe they are not worthy, capable, or spiritual enough to fulfill their true calling and God-given destiny. This book is not only encouraging and empowering for women, it is rich with the truth of God's Word. Thank you, Pam, for this important book."

—**Shirley Rose,** Total Living Network TV, and author of *Significant Living*

"Pam Farrel is a confidence builder! She helps a woman move from hopes and dreams right into the reality of living out God's best adventure for her life. Move into the life you've longed for with *Woman of Confidence.*"

—**Carole Lewis,** National Director, First Place 4 Health

WOMAN of CONFIDENCE

Pam Farrel

HARVEST HOUSE PUBLISHERS

EUGENE, OREGON

Published in association with the literary agency of Alive Communications, Inc., 7680 Goddard Street, Ste #200, Colorado Springs, CO 80920.

Cover by Left Coast Design, Portland, Oregon

Cover photo © Fancy Photography / Veer

WOMAN OF CONFIDENCE
Copyright © 2009 by Pam Farrel
Published by Harvest House Publishers
Eugene, Oregon 97402
www.harvesthousepublishers.com

Library of Congress Cataloging-in-Publication Data
Farrel, Pam, 1959-
Woman of confidence / Pam Farrel.—[Rec. ed.].
   p. cm.
ISBN 978-0-7369-2409-2 (pbk.)
1. Christian women—Religious life. 2. Success—Religious aspects—Christianity. 3. Confidence—Religious aspects—Christianity. I. Title.
BV4527.F49 2009
248.8'43—dc22

                                                                        2008036846

Printed in the United States of America

09 10 11 12 13 14 15 16 17 / BP-NI / 10 9 8 7 6 5 4 3 2 1

To all the women ready for God's adventure,
"all things are possible with God" (Mark 10:27).

To my husband, Bill, and my family,
thanks for being my adventure team.

To my friend and mentor, Vyonda,
I gained confidence because you lived out God's Word
every day in every way.
You taught us
how to live,
how to love,
and how to die.

Blessed are those who persevere under trial, because when they have stood the test, they will receive the crown of life that God has promised to those who love him.

And when the Chief Shepherd appears, you will receive the crown of glory that will never fade away.

"Be faithful, even to the point of death, and I will give you the crown of life."

James 1:12 (TNIV), 1 Peter 5:4, Revelation 2:10

Contents

Acknowledgments

I am so thankful for my Adventure Team. Thanks for going on the adventure with God and me. I want to thank my:

Awesomely wise and always supportive
husband, Bill

Devoted friendship circle and office team
in "The Joy Zone"

Very precise editor, Rod, who makes me
better than I am

Extra cooperative sons, Brock, Zach, and
Caleb, and daughter-in-law, Hannah

Nurturing Kathy, Faith, Tina, Sally, who
helped expand my view of God

Top-notch president of Harvest House
Publishers, Bob Hawkins Jr.

Unusually supportive marketing and
support team at Harvest House

Reliable prayer partner, best friend, and
adventure-team cheerleader, Robin

Energetic mom, Afton, who first nurtured
my adventure to write and speak

Terrific audiences who share their adventures
honestly so others can grow

Exceptional editor, Linda, who first planted
the seed for a book on confidence

Adorable Eden, a granddaughter who I pray
lives her God-sized adventure

Majestic God who loved me (and you)
enough to invite us on the adventure

It takes a team to reach God's adventure, and I am forever grateful to be surrounded by such an amazing, intelligent, encouraging team. I am a better leader because of those who surround me. This book is a culmination of years of living on the edge, trying to believe God for who He says He is, and being surrounded by people who tell me the truth about God, the truth about myself, and the truth about life and my writing and speaking. Jesus says, "The truth will set you free" (John 8:32), and I have been free to soar because of those who are the safety net under me and the adventure God has given to me. Thanks for holding the net.

Confident Living

*T*oday, as you pick up this book, you want to feel confident, courageous, or maybe even adventurous, but deep down a nagging fear stands in your way. Perhaps most of the day you feel your confidence level is up, but there is a person, a confidence killer, in your world who has the knack of sucking the wind right out of your sails. Circumstances or challenges can be confidence killers too. Maybe right now you have what feels like an insurmountable, impenetrable, or unmovable obstacle in the middle of the path to your adventure. Just taking stock of the situation is eroding your once confident heart.

Don't give up. The best, boldest, biggest adventure of your life might be just around the bend of your life if we can together garner the courage to forge forward. Confidence is not stolen. It is given away, and you, my dear friend, can get yours back or discover a new confidence you never knew existed!

CONFIDENCE CREATED

As I write this, I am approximately 30,000 feet over the Pacific Ocean traveling to Singapore to speak at the National Marriage

Conference sponsored by the government of Singapore. Bill and I were first invited when someone holding a high cabinet post read our book *Single Men Are Like Waffles, Single Women Are Like Spaghetti* and invited us to speak to university students and career singles. The following year, we were invited back to speak to couples to help strengthen marriages and families.

Does it surprise me that God has this assignment for me? Yes and no.

Yes, because I sure didn't start out to be a marriage and relationship specialist with my sights set on traveling the world. No, my world began small—very small. I was born in a town of less than a hundred people. I grew up on a sheep farm in southeast Idaho where going the 30 miles to town to grocery shop was such a big deal that we dressed up for the trip. The church where I heard about God's love averaged about 35 adults each Sunday. There was only one business in my hometown: a grocery store/post office/bait and tackle/car repair shop all rolled into one. And if I remember correctly, we did have a stop sign at the center of town.

However, my world grew and expanded. My father began to be successful, and we moved to larger homes in larger cities. He got bigger job titles, nicer cars, and more ritzy offices—until he made some unwise relationship choices that ended my parents' marriage.

The divorce was hard on all of us. It was the first time in my life I discovered that sometimes God uses pain as a motivator to get us to move "from strength to strength" (Psalm 84:7). My mother moved back to a single-wide trailer with three kids and bravely started all over again. I watched her daily face down her fears to forge out a better, stronger life for our family. In many ways my world was once again small, comfortable, cozy, and predictable—for a while.

God has some amazing things in store for us
if we're willing to walk into those
plans and adventures for our lives.

God knew He needed to teach me how to walk courageously, confidently, and boldly into the plan He had for me. God has some amazing things in store for us if we're willing to walk into those plans and adventures for our lives.

- Jesus came that we might experience life "to the full" (John 10:10).

- The apostle Paul, quoting from Isaiah, affirms that "No eye has seen, no ear has heard, no mind has conceived what God has prepared for those who love him" (1 Corinthians 2:9).

- Peter exclaims, "His divine power has given us everything we need for life and godliness through our knowledge of him who called us by his own glory and goodness. Through these he has given us his very great and precious promises, so that through them you may participate in the divine nature and escape the corruption in the world caused by evil desires" (2 Peter 1:3-4).

As I review these verses over and over, it doesn't surprise me that God has allowed me to travel to many of the world's continents to teach and speak. At eight years of age I was introduced to a God who said outrageous things He has consistently followed through on. He made promises such as:

"I came to give life to the full"…and He has.

"I can do exceedingly more than you can ask, think, dream, or feel"…and He does.

"Go into all the world and preach the gospel, and I will be with you wherever you go"…and He is with me.

"I will give you the words"…and He does, right down to the last syllable.

"With Christ, you are more than a conqueror"…and He has won many battles on my behalf.

"With my God I can leap a wall"…and He has helped me over all kinds of hurdles. I believe He will be true to His promises again and again if I'm willing to watch Him be Himself on my behalf for His greater reasons.

When I said "Yes" to Jesus and asked Him into my heart over 40 years ago, I signed up for an adventure with God. In my wide-eyed youthful innocence, I would read some traits and truths about God, and I would actually *believe* He was who He said He'd be. I would read a promise in the Bible and actually believe God meant to keep it, so I planned my life around it. As a result, I grew to believe God did love me. I saw Him in action. He did have a wonderful plan for my life. He was trustworthy then, so I can trust Him to be faithful again today, tomorrow, and the next day.

The more I gained a track record of trust in God, the easier it became to be confident. Courage is knit one thread at a time. Like a safety net under a high-wire tightrope walker, the safety net of God's love and character is under my life. *God's* character is *my* confidence. I think that's the secret truth in this verse:

> Such confidence as this is ours through Christ before God. Not that we are competent in ourselves to claim anything for ourselves, but our competence comes from God (2 Corinthians 3:4-5).

The principle becomes even clearer as you read it again in other translations of the Bible:

> Such confidence we have through Christ toward God. Not that we are adequate in ourselves to consider anything as coming from ourselves, but our adequacy is from God (NASB).

> Such is the confidence that we have through Christ toward God. Not that we are sufficient in ourselves to claim anything as coming from us, but our sufficiency is from God (ESV).

> We are confident of all this because of our great trust in God through Christ. It is not that we think we are

qualified to do anything on our own. Our qualification comes from God (NLT).

Convinced yet? Read on. My job in this book is to share God with you in such a way that *all of who He is* becomes available to help you live out *all that He is calling you to do*. Your mission is to read, learn, and discover who God is. Then it is God's job to be who He claims to be in His Word. As you learn to rely on who He is in your life rather than solely trust in your abilities, you can rest, relax, and run in His plan. Confidence will become a natural, normal way to live life.

I believe this is one of the most important skills we women need to develop. So if you are one of the millions of women who, like me (and like all your friends, if they're honest), have ever felt not-so-confident, that your past was nothing special and your future seems unclear, then *Woman of Confidence* is for you.

I will seek to change your thinking about life by looking at the lives of real women—women who have achieved because they relied upon God and followed His standards, His character, His strengths rather than their own. Within these pages we will investigate the principles to help you STEP into the adventure God has for your life.

The book is divided into four sections, each building on the other, to help you move STEP by STEP into your adventure. When I looked back on how God moved me from nothing into the adventure I am living today, I see the methods or proven skills He used to motivate me forward. As I look around at others who are successful, I see they have implemented these same skills as well. Using the STEP method will move you forward in life if you:

> **S**peak the adventure
> **T**eam up for the adventure
> **E**nergize the adventure
> **P**ush the adventure

God is preparing a way for you to STEP into the winner's circle of life. Each chapter will prepare you a little more for confident living. As you travel through the pages of this book, keep a journal handy. God is going to give you the information to win at life and love. It will be winning defined by His character, His standards, and His adventures for you, which will be a win that cannot fail because it is based on who God is, not just who you are.

SECURING THE WIN

Toward the end of each chapter you'll discover *Winning Words*—portions of Scripture strung together and personalized so that you can wrap your heart around the power of God's Word. You can add your own winning words by recording your favorite verses in your journal as personal encouragement from God's heart to your own. You can also use *Winning Words* to pray for yourself and others when they need confidence.

Each chapter will also have a section called *Winning Wisdom*, which includes an application of practical tools successful, confident women utilize to achieve their adventure.

Finally, each chapter ends with *Winning Ways*, accountability partner exercises and questions to keep "iron sharpening iron." Accountability partners are "fine-tuning" friends because they tune up your life to make a beautiful melody. So, before you jump in, contact a friend, or a few, and ask them to buy this book and make the journey to confidence together. (For an additional small-group Bible study for this book, go to www.farrelcommunications.com).

Sally Berger says, "The secret of getting ahead is getting started." The sooner you implement the principles, the sooner God can weave integrity, confidence, and achievement into your life. I pray that this book will point you to the character of God and be the catalyst you need to become a woman of confidence.

Ready to STEP into the adventure God has for you? Let's get started!

STEP into God's Adventure

Speak the Adventure
Team up for the Adventure
Energize the Adventure
Push the Adventure

Speak of the Adventure

Stepping Confidently...or Not

*"You can't, God never said you could.
God can, He always said He would."*

JILL BRISCOE

When we were newlyweds, my husband and I were challenged to leave our thriving youth ministry, our cozy church, and our longtime friends and head off to seminary. I didn't want to go. I cried for hours the night we were challenged to uproot and move. The seminary was located in the heart of Los Angeles, and for me, a farm girl, living in the suburbs had been a stretch. I saw Los Angeles as a hostile environment. I wasn't even sure God existed in Los Angeles.

But I knew I couldn't live with the stress I was feeling. I couldn't go around with swollen eyes from crying, a sullen attitude, or the feeling of fear and dread that accompanied me like a black cloud. In addition, I knew I couldn't let my fears keep me from God's best plan for Bill and me. I never want to live a life of regrets or "if onlys" or "I wish I would haves." I wanted to be the kind of woman who could grab God's brass ring as I rode the merry-go-round of life. But I was petrified and paralyzed by my fears.

So I made a list of women who I thought were confident. Then I called one. Barbara was the mother of one of my best friends. Barbara had been around the world, accompanying her husband to dangerous and exotic countries, with three tiny children in tow. I thought if anyone knew how to make the pain inside my heart go away, she would. (And I was secretly hoping she'd say, "Oh, sweetie, you're right. I'm sure God's not calling you into a hostile place like Los Angeles.")

I showed up at Barbara's home at three o'clock in the afternoon and didn't leave until nine that evening. To my surprise, Barbara didn't take my side. Instead, she confirmed my calling. And then she went one step further—hour after hour, example after example, she walked me through the character of God and His faithfulness in her life. Over dinner at a local restaurant, Barbara recounted to me the faithfulness of God in her life. And as we returned to her home, Barbara continued to recount to me the faithfulness of God.

That night when my husband came to pick me up, I walked through the doors of Barbara's home with confidence, knowing I could walk through any door God opened. I embraced God's faithfulness and unchanging character, and I felt like a new woman—a woman of confidence.

Barbara spoke the adventure into my heart initially, and then I chose to speak the adventure: *Pam, you and God can handle this move and any future move God has for you.*

A New Attitude

Women—people—are desperate for confidence. A quick perusal of the Internet produces hundreds of sites for building self-esteem. "All in all, we are not very confident by nature. Ninety percent of our thoughts about ourselves are negative," says Alice Domar, Ph.D., director of the Mind/Body Center for Women's Health at Harvard Medical School. It has been estimated that almost 90 percent of college students feel inferior in some way.

Focus on the Family's James Dobson once said, "If I could write a prescription for the women of this world, I would provide each of them with a healthy dose of self-esteem and personal worth (taken three times a day until the symptoms disappear). I have no doubt this is their greatest need."

Self-defeating behavior is the single most common reason that people seek psychotherapy, according to Mark Goulston, M.D. Dr. Goulston explains that some of us are raised to be more confident than others: "If when things go wrong for a child their parents respond angrily or fearfully, they're more likely to grow up feeling...insecure." Lack of confidence seriously affects a majority of women.

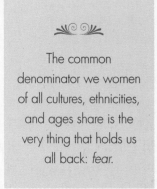

The common denominator we women of all cultures, ethnicities, and ages share is the very thing that holds us all back: *fear.*

Our self-confidence is so fragile that according to a Yale University researcher's study, even a bad-hair day affects us. On those bad-hair days we feel less smart, less capable, more embarrassed, and less sociable.

CONFIDENCE KILLERS

For the past ten years I have been surveying women from the audiences I have spoken to. One of the questions I ask is: "What holds you back from saying, 'I will take on that cause, that ministry, that opportunity, or that person and mentor her'? What holds you back?"

In every audience I always get the exact same response: Every time, on every continent, in every country and every city. The common denominator we women of all cultures, ethnicities, and ages share is the very thing that holds us all back: *fear.*

- Fear of failure
- Fear of success
- Fear of what others think
- Fear of feeling inadequate for the task

- Fear of criticism
- Fear of not feeling smart enough, thin enough, young enough, mature enough

It's all fear based. The reason most of us are not living out our adventure is fear.

AM I LOSING IT HERE?

During the two years I was researching this book, I took inventory of confidence killers by asking two simple questions of those in my audiences and in my daily world:

1. What stops you in your tracks or sucks the confidence right out of you?
2. What do you do to rebuild it?

These women ranged from the average woman who may never describe herself as confident to bold leaders who were accustomed to taking risks. I was impressed that they were willing to pull back the curtain to their hearts and share their underlying fears. The easiest way to categorize these fears is to picture what women are afraid of losing. Here in ascending order (from least frequent to most frequent) are the confidence killers I uncovered:

Loss of salvation: Fears that a spouse, a child, a parent or other loved one, or we ourselves will choose not to acknowledge or embrace God or faith.

Loss of health: Fear of aging and illness—given how infrequently this was mentioned, not many fear loss of health until it actually happens.

Loss of security: Fears of losing our money, our home—our comfort zone.

Loss of control: Fear of the future—fear that life was too busy, too big, or too complicated to handle with the skills or resources we believe we have (or don't have).

Loss of relationship with God: This one surprised me because I speak to audiences filled with women who claim to walk with God. Yet many have a hidden fear of disappointing that same God. These women carry a belief that God would never leave them, but they wrestle with the fear that if they really are as inadequate and imperfect as they feel, God will bail on them. This is a fragile faith, a fractured foundation, that I hope this book will help fix.

Loss of a spouse: Those of us who are married simply cannot picture our lives apart from our husbands. This is actually not all bad. I love Bill so much that I feel we are truly one. We finish each other's sentences. We think as one many times. When we do presentations, we can select, without talking it over, what to cut and know the other would make the same choice. We are so "one" it's as if our names are BillandPamFarrel.

However, reality forces us women to face down this fear because most women will outlive their mate. Equal numbers of women named the fear of loss of spouse by divorce, not just loss by death. Many women voiced fears that their husbands would find someone younger, sexier, smarter, richer, or simply more "available."

Loss of community: Fears of being alone, rejected, ignored, friendless.

Loss of a child: By nature we believe our kids should bury us, not the other way around. Surprisingly, many women also express the fear of losing a child to rebellion. Many asked me to pray for a prodigal child, often a teen caught in an immoral lifestyle or trapped by drugs or alcohol.

Loss of status: Overwhelmingly (three to one), the most common fear included anything that makes us look bad in public. Loss of reputation, loss of status, or things that might cause us public humiliation topped the list of fears. In days past, if an error in judgment happened, we might have to face wagging fingers in our hometown, but there was the hope that we might be able to move away and get a fresh start. In a world linked by the Internet, there are not many places left to hide from our humanity. To err is human, to erase from the hard drive is divine.

To move on from the fear of loss, we need to learn to voice our hopes and dreams, and then frame up the steps to move into the adventure.

SPEAK IT

So what is your dream? What are your hopes for the future? What is the adventure you secretly hope God has in store for you?

An adventure can be any hope, dream, passion, calling, or wish God has laid on your heart and planted in your soul. It can be a calling that is from any realm of life: business, ministry, social justice, personal growth so you can become a difference maker, or even a relationship goal. An adventure is *an exciting or extraordinary event or series of events and an undertaking involving uncertainty and risk*. You won't know the details of the adventure—that's what makes it an adventure. Just paint it with bold broad brush strokes and let God fill in the rest as you journey together.

Furthermore, you might have more than one adventure on your heart. What is burning in your soul today? Take the first step and say what it is. Say it again out loud. Name it. Speak it, girlfriend. Then write in the space below who you want to be in five to ten years; describe the woman you'd like to become:

Now write what you picture that woman doing, saying, living:

Now tell someone. Tell a person who believes in you, believes in God, and wants God's very best for your life. Tell someone who you think will pray for you, cheer for you, support and encourage you to be all God designed you to be. There is power in the speaking. Speak the adventure!

One of my friends is now a successful television personality. When she was fresh out of college, she announced to the sixth-grade girls she was teaching in Sunday school that someday they would see her on TV. Once she spoke it, she felt compelled to walk out that dream in order to be a woman of integrity to those young impressionable minds. She confessed to me that had she not spoken that dream aloud to those young women, she might have given up that dream. Speaking the adventure, the dream, holds us accountable to at least try for the adventure.

Speaking the adventure helps you define what God and you will team up to do and what you will then choose *not* to do. You will need to listen clearly for God's voice and keep it above all other voices. In future chapters, I will help you gain skills to tune up your heart to hear God's voice above all others. As you hear God's voice, speak out what you believe God is telling you. You need to hear those truths to gain inner courage.

God knows the true power of speaking an adventure. In numerous places in His Word, He commands us to confess, proclaim, and speak the goodness and greatness of God. I think God knows we need to hear the truth in our minds and through our ears. Speaking it drowns out negative thoughts such as, *Who do you think you are? What do you think you're doing? You've got to be kidding. You?*

Instead, God encourages us to speak up and speak out.

> LORD, who may dwell in your sanctuary?
>   Who may live on your holy hill?
> He whose walk is blameless
>   and who does what is righteous,
> who speaks the truth from his heart
>   and has no slander on his tongue...
> He who does these things
>   will never be shaken.
>
> (Psalm 15: 1-3,5)

He who walks righteously
and speaks what is right...
this is the man who will dwell on the heights,
whose refuge will be the mountain fortress.
His bread will be supplied,
and water will not fail him.

(Isaiah 33:15-16)

We will not hide them from their children;
we will tell the next generation
the praiseworthy deeds of the LORD,
his power, and the wonders he has done...
so the next generation would know them,
even the children yet to be born,
and they in turn would tell their children.
Then they would put their trust in God
and would not forget his deeds
but would keep his commands.
They would not be like their forefathers—
a stubborn and rebellious generation.

(Psalm 78:4,6-8)

While speaking out the truth is powerful, it is important to realize *why* it is powerful and what the focus needs to be. The strength of speaking the dream is not in your personality, pleading, or power. Just because you speak your adventure doesn't mean it will happen. But if you speak *God's adventure* over your life, then all of who God is will be working in your direction. The key to figuring out His adventure for your life is to try to think more like God. That is really the core message of this book. It is a tool to help you learn more about God and hear His truths. The more you practice, the more natural it will become to view yourself and your life from God's point of view.

Walk in Adventure

The essence of confidence is grabbing hold of God's hand and walking out His plan. The power rests solely in connecting to God and getting on God's page and plan for your life. By speaking His truths, standing on His promises, and proclaiming His character, the inner ability to live confidently blossoms. As you get to know God and the truths God speaks over you, you will begin to think more like God. When you think more like the Holy One who created you, you will make better, wiser decisions and choices, and with each good, solid decision, you will gain confidence.

> If I submerge myself in who God is and in His truths, I will begin to think like God about my life. His desires will become my desires, and my desires will be lined up with His plans.

When I was a college freshman, my mentor introduced me to a verse I have tried to make my goal each day:

> Delight yourself in the LORD
> and he will give you the desires of your heart.
>
> (Psalm 37:4)

If I submerge myself in who God is and in His truths, I will begin to think like God about my life. His desires will become my desires, and my desires will be lined up with His plans. The goal is to be one heart with God. Then you can step out in confidence, sensing God is right there with you.

Free, Free, Free at Last

One of the verses that has given me the ability to gain courage and confidence is a simple sentence, but once you get your heart wrapped around it, you are freed from others' perceptions and expectations and gain the ability to perform for an audience of

One—God. "You will know the truth and the truth will set you free" (John 8:32).

Throughout this book, you will hear a wealth of truths about yourself, your life, and God's adventure for you. As you embrace those truths and give up the negative self-talk and Satan's lies and the toxic dysfunctional phrases you may have accumulated along life's path, you will discover the ability to be courageous even under the most stressful, impossible situations.

> If I have been feeding my heart with God's truths, I am not as afraid because God's truths about Himself and His power and ability fill my mind.

Later on this path to your adventure, I will equip you with tools to battle such confidence killers. As you gain more tools, your confidence will build and you will discover the adventure life has to offer when viewed from God's point of view.

Your confidence may feel unreal at times. That's because it won't be yours; it will be the gift God gives to you that is wrapped in His truths.

Sometimes people ask me if I'm afraid to speak to a crowd of important people or meet leaders with big names or travel to a foreign country alone.

If I have been feeding my heart with God's truths, I am not as afraid because God's truths about Himself and His power and ability fill my mind. But if I focus on the circumstance, the possibility of failure or harm, then I am petrified. If I feed into God's view of me and my life, I gain courage. If I do not stoke the fires of confidence by focusing on God, I slide back down into my cesspool of fears.

THE KEY TO CONFIDENCE

So what is the key to confidence? What unlocks a person's potential without harming the person's psyche? What is the secret to real success, staying power, and fulfillment? How can we achieve, maybe achieve greatly, and still maintain our integrity? What builds courage in our heart that is played out in action in our world? How can we develop the confidence to walk into our hopes, dreams, aspirations, and our adventure with God?

> Nothing is more vital, more central to your
> self-confidence than your confidence in God.

Confident women think differently. They think differently because they think different thoughts—not their own, but God's. The confidence of their life is rooted in the most primary of all relationships—a relationship with God. We can become women of confidence only as we grasp a great view of God.

A.W. Tozer says in his classic book, *The Knowledge of the Holy*, "What comes into our minds when we think about God is the most important thing about us." Henry Blackaby and Claude King agree. In *Experiencing God*, they write, "How I live my life is a testimony of what I believe about God."

I like to say, "Show me your God, and I will show you your ability to achieve. Small God—small life. Big God—big opportunities and potential await." Too many of us, however, do not see God for who He really is. J.B. Phillips, in *Your God Is Too Small*, explains the quandary many of us find ourselves in:

> We are modeling God upon what we know of man. That is why it is contended here that what at first sight appears to be almost a super adequate idea of God is, in reality, inadequate—it is based on too tiny a foundation. Man may be made in the image of God; but it is not sufficient to conceive God as nothing more than infinitely magnified man.[1]

Beth Moore, in *A Taste of Believing God*, writes, "Who we believe God is greatly affects our eternal destinies, but I'd like to suggest that nothing has a greater effect on the quality of our lives and the fulfillment of our destinies…we're wise to ask ourselves the question, Who do I say God is?"[2]

Jesus asked those who followed Him that same question:

> Then he asked them, "But who do you say I am?"
>
> Simon Peter answered, "You are the Messiah, the Son of the living God."
>
> Jesus replied, "You are blessed, Simon son of John, because my Father in heaven has revealed this to you. You did not learn this from any human being. Now I say to you that you are Peter…and upon this rock I will build my church, and all the powers of hell will not conquer it. And I will give you the keys of the Kingdom of Heaven. Whatever you forbid on earth will be forbidden in heaven, and whatever you permit on earth will be permitted in heaven" (Matthew 16:15-19 NLT).

I remember in college coming across this passage, "I know whom I have believed, and am convinced that he is able to guard what I have entrusted to him for that day" (2 Timothy 1:12).

A richer translation of this verse might read, "I know whom I have believed and am still believing and am convinced and am still convinced that He is able to guard what I have deposited with Him." Don't you love that picture? We each decide to deposit our belief in Christ, and it builds interest as we keep believing and keep being convinced of His ability. So how do we make a deposit into Christ First Ability Bank? Make a decision, and then walk it out, over and over and over.

Seeing God as merely an elevated form of ourselves sets us up for failure. We miss out on all God has for us because we fail to see Him as the all-powerful, all-knowing, all-loving God who provides for all our needs. But when we examine God's unchanging character, we gain confidence in Him and in His love for us. We become confident that He will work in and through us. When we walk that out every day of our lives, we become more confident than the day before.

THE SHORTCUT COMES UP SHORT

Ann came to me one day very upset. It seems Susan, one of her employees who was also a good friend, was on the verge of a nervous breakdown. Susan, wanting to achieve and get ahead in life, had been overdosing on self-help motivational tapes. Over and over again she was told, "You can do it. You can do it." In reality Susan couldn't do it. "It" was causing her to lose her mind. Instead of feeling better about herself, she had become severely depressed and was on the brink of a collapse.

Ann and I chatted a few moments about the positive benefits of a deep relationship with God as the source of strength, confidence, and success in life. She began to dig in and learn who God was and how she could know Him better. Today Ann has a deep relationship with God, and He has blessed her with a successful business and healthy relationships with friends and family.

Susan, however, rebuffed Ann's biblically centered advice and went on to become "her own god," as she put it. She relied on herself and others to give her confidence and strength. As a result, Susan has left in her wake a trail of broken people, broken relationships, and broken promises.

It is possible by ourselves to seek confidence and achievement— at least symbols of achievement such as titles, power, money, and possessions—but miss inner contentment. And it is possible to have all the perks of achievement and feel great about ourselves, but we may be the only ones who feel that way because we have used and stepped on people to get what we want. Anything short of God's view on life and we shortcut the very character we need to achieve. True achievement exists only when our confidence comes from God and our gain results from a life of integrity.

THE REWARDS OF CONFIDENCE

A godly woman with a heart of integrity not only has confidence, she inspires confidence. With that confidence comes achievement, not only in this world but, more important, in the one beyond—a world where God has rewards waiting for us that will make any benefit package here on earth pale in comparison.

This book is dedicated to my friend Vyonda Benson, a woman who achieved with integrity and inspired with her achievement.

A godly woman with a heart of integrity not only has confidence, she inspires confidence.

Vyonda survived the Depression, the Dust Bowl, and many economic downturns. She married young, partly to escape a raging, violent father. She bore four children, and then her husband was diagnosed with crippling arthritis and was retired early by his company due to his disability. But because of her faith in God, Vyonda was confident that He would provide. With only a ninth-grade education, Vyonda and her family started their own business. As a couple, she and her husband, Mel, planted the church my husband eventually pastored for 15 years.

Over the years I knew Vyonda, I never heard her complain. She didn't complain about pain, trials, finances, people—she didn't complain. Instead, Vyonda had a quiet confidence and a steady faith. She successfully sailed through some deep waters and storms because she knew God.

Just hours before her death, in a quiet moment in her bedroom, I held the frail body of my dear brave friend so she could breathe just a bit better. I sang to her hymns of the faith, knowing that she had achieved much here on earth, but her best rewards were still ahead. I am convinced that as she stepped across eternity's threshold, she heard, "Well done, my good and faithful servant." The mark of true confidence is the conviction that, at the end of your life, you can confidently enter through those pearl-studded gates and hear God proclaim from the throne, "Well done."

Some motivational leaders say that the woman in the mirror is her own goddess, the master of her destiny. But I know all my imperfections and shortcomings. I am utterly human. I do not want to rely on my own strength and power. I want to rely on something—Someone—who is all-powerful, all-knowing, all-loving. I want to achieve by seeing God clearly through understanding His Word and through living life based upon that grand glimpse of the majestic.

Confidence Can Be Yours

It was one of those days. It must have been a Monday. I had been away at speaking engagements all weekend, and when I picked up the phone to listen to my messages, the automated voice blared in my ear, "You have 31 messages." I slammed down the receiver and turned on my computer to retrieve my e-mail. "You've got mail. You've got mail. You've got mail." I looked across my desk. Stacks of correspondence needed answers, and a half-written manuscript and research books created a tower of pressing priorities. I let out a long, frustrated sigh. I was officially overwhelmed.

I had made a previous commitment to God that I wouldn't start my work day unless I'd first spent time with Him. And this day I'd jumped the gun.

I reached across my desk for my dog-eared copy of *Daily Light on the Daily Path*, a book that gathers verses of the Bible together by topic into daily readings. The day was January 8, so I opened the book to that date and read:

> I know whom I have believed and am persuaded that He is able. Able to do exceedingly abundantly above all that we ask or think. Able to make all grace abound toward you, that you, always having all sufficiency in all things, may have an abundance for every good work. Able to aid those who are tempted. Able to save to the uttermost those who come to God through Him, since He always lives to make intercession for them. Able to keep you from stumbling, and to present you faultless before the presence of His glory with exceeding joy. Able to keep what I have

committed to Him until that day. Who will transform our lowly body that it may be conformed to His glorious body, according to the working by which He is able even to subdue all things to Himself. "Do you believe I am able to do this?" They said to Him, "Yes, Lord." "According to your faith let it be to you."[3]

Able, able, able. I felt free to be me and let God be God. He was able. I didn't have to do it all and be it all. He could enable me to carry out what He deemed vital from His perspective—and He'd help me to see exactly what that would be.

Being so encouraged by this devotional, I immediately thought of my other friends in various places of leadership who might also be encouraged by it. I reopened the devotional to copy it. I opened to January 8...and it wasn't there. I thought maybe I had mistakenly opened to February 8, but it wasn't there either. No, it was the March 8 devotional I had read. My God is so able that He led me to read the wrong date's reading on the right day for me. He is able.

You too will find that He is able, and with that knowledge, you will become a woman of confidence.

WINNING WORDS

When you struggle with confidence, review and pray these verses out loud:

> For you have been my hope, O Sovereign LORD, my confidence since my youth. I have no fear of sudden disaster or of the ruin that overtakes the wicked, for the LORD will be my confidence and will keep my foot from being snared. In him and through faith in him I may approach God with freedom and confidence. I am confident of this, that he who began a good work in me will carry it on to completion until the day of Christ Jesus. I will approach the throne of grace with confidence, so that I may receive mercy and find grace to help me in my time of need. This

is the confidence I have in approaching God: that if I ask anything according to his will, he hears me. And if I know that he hears me—whatever I ask—I know that I have what I asked of him. Therefore, brothers, since I have confidence to enter the Most Holy Place by the blood of Jesus, by a new and living way opened for me through the curtain, that is, his body, and since I have a great priest over the house of God, I will draw near to God with a sincere heart in full assurance of faith, having my heart sprinkled to cleanse me from a guilty conscience. I will hold unswervingly to the hope I profess, for he who promised is faithful.

WINNING WISDOM

When are you least confident? I used to lose confidence when I received a phone message from someone I deemed important. I used to go into a tailspin thinking I must have disappointed him or her in some way, and I would think this before I even knew what the message was about. I would always go to the negative conjecture first. This was totally an irrational thought linked back to being a child of an alcoholic father and never seeming to please him. As I studied God's character as a father, however, this unconfident behavior has nearly dissolved away. By gazing into one of God's traits, I regained my momentum in life. For me it was learning to see God as my loving daddy.

What's yours? What causes you to lose confidence? Your boss's look? Your spouse's response? New situations? The learning curve? A difficult person? Life not going your way? Feeling like everything is changing too fast to keep up?

Write a letter to God in your journal, naming the confidence killers in your life. Then choose one and ask, "What name of God, trait of God, attribute of God, can I trade my fear for?" Try to think of what is the opposite of that fear and see if there's a corresponding trait of God that is a place you can hang your heart. Then go to Biblegateway.com (or another Bible program) and plug in this trait of God and find a favorite verse that makes you regain your confidence when you read it, say it, and hear it. Now post it in a prominent place and speak it until you know it by heart. Talk to God and ask Him to help you focus not on your shortcomings but on His power and ability. Then watch your confidence grow.

WINNING WAYS

Think of one or two girlfriends you can trust with your dream. Buy an extra copy (or a few) of this book, then ask her (or them) to meet with you once a week or once a month, whatever your schedules allow, and be each others' adventure cheerleaders. Set up your first coffee time, walk and talk, or lunch date. Share your answers to the questions from the "Winning Wisdom" section.

2

Stride to the Dream

The First Few Steps

> "Heat is required to forge anything.
> Every great accomplishment is the
> story of a flaming heart."
>
> MARY LOU RETTON

The applause erupted. People were shouting, standing, and whistling appreciation for the slim ballerina in white. But as they placed the crown upon her head, she couldn't hear the applause or even the congratulations. Heather Whitestone, crowned Miss America 1995, couldn't hear the well-wishing applause because she is deaf.

Most people don't realize that the steps to that Miss America crown were long, painful, and repeated. Many hurdles had to be overcome. Most of us would never have hung in there, especially when nearly everyone said Heather's dream would never be a reality.

My son Caleb runs hurdles in track. One is the 300-meter race, which is a long race for a hurdler. It is common for hurdlers to trip over the last few hurdles due to exhaustion, but those who have trained well glide over the final hurdles because they are accustomed to the rigors of the race. In the same way, God often has us hurdling a few obstacles to better prepare us to live out the adventure once we cross the finish line.

GET IN STRIDE

Hurdlers work on keeping in stride over each hurdle by acting as if it is just one big step. This helps them stay in rhythm and on pace. When striding toward your dream, make it your goal to stay in stride with God despite the obstacles that appear in your path.

Let's look back at Heather's race to the crown. When Heather was a toddler, her mother dropped a set of pans in the kitchen and realized that Heather could not hear. While other children played, Heather worked to learn to read lips and pronounce words correctly. Determined to live a normal life, Heather attended a public school where she was the only deaf student. But she was unable to keep up with her class work and began to fall behind her peers.

Heather needed a haven, and so for three years she attended a school for the deaf in St. Louis, far from her home in the South. But when she returned to public school, Heather felt alone. "My loneliness was eased, though, because at that time I discovered what it meant to have a personal relationship with Jesus Christ."

Heather also found solace in dance. In early elementary school, frustrated with the inability to communicate, she began ballet class and discovered a safe emotional harbor. Heather explains her love of dance in the book *Listening with My Heart:*

> Dancing is a natural, expressive way to bring praise and glory to God. I had first come to this conclusion on Christmas Eve when I was very young. I waited until everyone in the house went to bed, then I slipped into the living room and turned on the Christmas tree lights. Caught by the wonder and the spirit of Christmas, I pretended to be the Virgin Mary. With a baby doll we used to represent the infant Jesus, I danced around the tree, offering my dance as a celebratory gift to God. It became my secret, personal tradition which I repeated every year, and I always felt that God enjoyed it tremendously.[1]

THE DREAM IS SET

I believe that God used that first dance around the tree, performed just for Jesus, to set the dream in Heather's heart. Heather knew the race God had called her to run. However, just because the dream is planted doesn't mean it is automatically going to happen. Often God allows great obstacles along the path so that once the dream comes to fruition, we value and appreciate God more and the dream more. Overcoming obstacles is also God's training program so we gain the wisdom and stamina to live out the dream.

> God is the master of taking dark and turning it into light; taking bad and bending it into good; taking seeming misfortune and making it into fortunate opportunity.

Heather had a few hurdles too. Like most teens, Heather wanted to fit in, but she also wanted to be the best at something. "Because I wanted to have something special to show my children, I decided to enter my first pageant—the Shelby County Junior Miss program. Even though I didn't win—I was second runner-up—this was a great experience because it brought me out of my isolation and helped me relate to girls my own age."

KEEPING YOUR STRIDE

One way to keep your stride and sail over life's hurdles is to look for the silver lining amidst life's storms. Silver linings are not difficult for God. In fact, He promises to create silver linings out of the worst of days. Romans 8:28 and 31 say it best, "And we know that in all things God works for the good of those who love him, who have been called according to his purpose…What, then, shall we say in response to this? If God is for us, who can be against us?"

God is the master of taking dark and turning it into light; taking bad and bending it into good; taking seeming misfortune and making it into fortunate opportunity. Chuck Swindoll says that "we are all faced with a series of great opportunities that are often brilliantly disguised as impossible situations."[2]

What are you facing that seems like an impossible situation? What obstacle is standing between you and the dream you believe God has for your life? What is stealing your confidence, joy, and fulfillment in life? Look for God's silver lining.

I hear what you're probably thinking. *Sure, Pollyanna Pam, I'll put on my rose-colored glasses and get right to the chorus of the musical* Annie. *In fact, I'll dream the impossible dream and sing that "sun will come out tomorrow" tune, and tap my ruby red slippers three times and wish my way to somewhere over the rainbow. Get real, Pam.*

Okay, I know it takes more than singing show tunes when faced with an impossible situation (but that is one creative way to get an attitude adjustment). Let me take you on a step-by-step approach to your adventure and help you hurdle those obstacles in your path.

Tell the Truth

I start with admitting that the situation looks bad. But I also know that God is good. I usually throw in a verse or two that I've memorized, such as Psalm 84:11 (NASB):

> For the LORD God is a sun and shield;
> The LORD gives grace and glory;
> No good thing does He withhold from those
> who walk uprightly.

Thomas Edison once said, "Opportunity is missed by most people because it is dressed in overalls and looks like work."[3] The hardest work is often trying to find the silver lining in a tough situation. A favorite activity I do when things look bleak is to string together verses on a topic and place them in a pretty frame or superimpose them on a beautiful picture, creating my own poster. During one particularly tough season—when I felt life was unfair, and we felt abandoned by some of those who we thought should have been walking alongside us—I knew I had a choice. I could stay swimming in that toxic waste of self-pity, and if I did, it would erode my faith, joy, and hope. It would also likely change my positive personality and make me a bitter, resentful woman. I didn't want that.

So I chose instead to make a list of all the verses that declare God's goodness, favor, and anointing. I prayed those verses over my life, over my husband and our family, personalizing them by placing our names right into the verses. By proclaiming God's goodness and giving God time to be good, our family soon saw the goodness of God.

I tell women who have had a storm hit their lives that it takes time for the ship to right itself. But if you keep pouring in the truth of God's Word, the truth will overwhelm the attack, and soon your ship will be sailing on smooth waters again, racing toward the finish line of the adventure. The truth helps you stay on course with God.

By focusing as a family on God's goodness, we were able to keep our attitude positive, and that kept our energy and motivation up. Because people want to invest in positive, proactive people, bigger and better opportunities soon presented themselves. Two of our sons received college scholarships; Bill was offered a better paying position at a more prestigious organization; we garnered several new contracts for books and DVDs; our audience sizes grew; and more media opportunities expanded our influence and platform, giving us the resources and tools we needed to help more people. Helping people is always God's goal for the adventure. The adventure doesn't just make you happy or provide for you and your family; God's adventure expands to helping others in some way too.

Because helping others is the goal of an adventure, the finish line is often the hardest thing to keep in view when obstacles arise. At one point in our family's trauma, I needed to remember that the mission statement of our ministry is "to bring practical insights to people's personal relationships." My personal pain was clouding my view, so I researched the number of new marriages in America each year and wrote those numbers on the whiteboard in my office. Underneath them I wrote, "Do not let the few (antagonists) keep you from reaching the 2.3 million for God."

Take on the Adversaries

One of my heroes in leadership is Nehemiah, a man who kept his confidence in a firestorm of criticism. I read Charles Swindoll's book about Nehemiah, *Two Steps Forward, Three Steps Back*, before my twenty-first birthday, and Nehemiah's example has spurred me forward through many a trying time since. In the story straight from the Bible (Nehemiah 2–6), Nehemiah has two rough critics, Sanballat and Tobiah, who mock and ridicule Nehemiah's effort to rebuild the wall around God's temple city, Jerusalem. But Nehemiah just keeps on working, not letting those two keep him from God's adventure for his life. Here's how he handled those critics:

Is someone or something distracting you from the adventure? Get your eyes off them and back on to the adventure.

> I answered them by saying, "The God of heaven will give us success. We his servants will start rebuilding, but as for you, you have no share in Jerusalem or any claim or historic right to it" (Nehemiah 2:20).

Chapter 3 lists all the repairs and headway the people made under Nehemiah's brave, focused leadership. Then the criticism got even more intense:

> But when Sanballat, Tobiah, the Arabs, the Ammonites and the men of Ashdod heard that the repairs to Jerusalem's walls had gone ahead and that the gaps were being closed, they were very angry. They all plotted together to come and fight against Jerusalem and stir up trouble against it (4:7).

Once again, Nehemiah responded with more focus on God and the dream at hand: "But we prayed to our God and posted a guard day and night to meet this threat" (4:9). Then he just kept on task, no matter the attack:

> Meanwhile, the people in Judah said, "The strength of the laborers is giving out, and there is so much rubble that we cannot rebuild the wall."
>
> Also our enemies said, "Before they know it or see us, we will be right there among them and will kill them and put an end to the work."
>
> Then the Jews who lived near them came and told us ten times over, "Wherever you turn, they will attack us."
>
> Therefore I stationed some of the people behind the lowest points of the wall at the exposed places, posting them by families, with their swords, spears and bows. After I looked things over, I stood up and said to the nobles, the officials and the rest of the people, "Don't be afraid of them. Remember the Lord, who is great and awesome, and fight for your brothers, your sons and your daughters, your wives and your homes" (4:10-14).

You have to admire that kind of positive focus. And of course God blessed it. In spite of the ongoing threats, Nehemiah and the rest of his workers completed the task:

> So the wall was completed on the twenty-fifth of Elul, in fifty-two days. When all our enemies heard about this, all the surrounding nations were afraid and lost their self-confidence, because they realized that this work had been done with the help of our God (6:15-16).

In the end, the critics were silenced by God. A huge celebration took place, and Israel moved back into a safe and secure city. Nehemiah prayed for favor from the Lord, stuck tenaciously to the task of working out the dream, and favor was granted.

Is someone or something distracting you from the adventure? Get your eyes off them and back on to the adventure.

STICKIN' TO IT

Heather Whitestone too had to keep sticking to the dream. Getting older didn't erase her longing to belong.

> Over and over I prayed, "God, who am I? Hearing or deaf?"...Negative thoughts seemed to badger my every waking thought and moment. Vaclav Havel once said, "There are times when we must sink to the bottom of our misery to understand truth, just as we must descend to the bottom of a well to see the stars in broad daylight"...But God brought me back from the edge of despair by guiding my reading of the Bible...Though I still didn't know where I'd find a place in this world, I knew that I was in capable hands: God's.
>
> Hearing God's voice in my heart and in his Word began opening up the whole world to me. One night I looked up at the stars and noticed that all the stars looked different. Later I discovered that the Bible says that even the stars differ from each other in their beauty and brightness (1 Cor. 15:41)...That truth is so comforting...God knows us better than we know ourselves. He knows our full potential, and he holds a bright, *realistic* dream for each one of us.

One evening during Heather's freshman year of college, she and her mother watched the Miss America pageant on TV. Heather was enthralled. "I want to have that opportunity...I want to perform my ballet on television," she told her mother.

Her mom's first response was to tally up the financial cost. She took on a second job in addition to her teaching job, and during the year Heather actively competed, her mom held down three jobs.

Heather competed in the Miss Alabama contest and only received first runner-up. Later she won a local pageant, made plans to return to the Miss Alabama contest, and committed herself to hours of studying, dance rehearsal, and community service.

Heading into her second Miss Alabama pageant, Heather was expected to win. As the announcement came, her name was announced as…first runner-up. Heather was astonished. *"No, not me.* As I walked to get my flowers and take the first runner-up position—for a second time—I thought, *How can I do this? How can I come so close and not win? What is wrong with me?"*

> When things get tough, I walk myself straight into God's throne room and take a good hard look at His character instead of the circumstances that surround me.

Heather decided not to try for the title a third time. But then she received a letter that changed her mind:

> I wanted you to know that a deaf man came to me looking for a job…I didn't know whether or not I should hire him until I saw you on stage. I watched how you mastered your situation and overcame your problems. I really admired your efforts, and because of your example, I decided to hire the deaf man and give him a chance.

Heather reflects on that day: "Even if you think you will never reach your dream, remember that you will learn something and touch others on the journey."

Trade in Your Perspective

When things get tough, I make myself set my tears and feelings aside for a moment. I walk myself straight into God's throne room and take a good hard look at His character instead of the circumstances that surround me. Then I say what I know to be true from the Bible. God is good, God is all-knowing, God is all-powerful, God is in control, and so on. I say the truth until I get a revised view on things and am ready to go back and hang on to my dream.

One of my favorite friends is high in the corporate world, and her "confidence killer" is when she is made to feel invisible. Here's how she's learned to handle this:

> I recall specific times in my life when I know that God chose me to do things way beyond my abilities and equipped me to do them. Then I thank Him for those opportunities and tell Him if He will use me again, He will clearly get all the glory because I surely cannot do it in my own strength or knowledge. When I am focused on Him and figuring out what He wants me to do, I get over feeling invisible. I try to remember to always pray for the people who made me feel that way.

My friend has faced down her fears, confidence killers, and obstacles to climb high on the ladder of success.

When you trade in your fear for the character of God, you'll gain a renewed hope and a personal peace. One of Heather Whitestone's favorite quotes is, "When we walk to the edge of all the light we have and step out into the darkness of the unknown, we must believe that there will be something solid to stand on or that we will be taught how to fly." I also wonder how high we could soar if we would only choose to fly on God's wings, saddled to His Spirit.

When we function from a heavenly perspective, we soon realize that no obstacle is too big for God. Nothing can stop His plan. Let's take a quick review of God's ability to carry a dream through to completion:

> Ah, Sovereign Lord, you have made the heavens and the earth by your great power and outstretched arm. Nothing is too hard for you (Jeremiah 32:17).

> His dominion is an eternal dominion;
>   his kingdom endures from generation to generation.

All the peoples of the earth
   are regarded as nothing.
He does as he pleases
   with the powers of heaven
   and the peoples of the earth.
No one can hold back his hand
   or say to him: "What have you done?"

(Daniel 4:34-35)

For nothing is impossible with God (Luke 1:37).

"I am the vine; you are the branches. If a man remains in me and I in him, he will bear much fruit; apart from me you can do nothing" (John 15:5).

The LORD Almighty has sworn,

   "Surely, as I have planned, so it will be,
      and as I have purposed, so it will stand."
For the LORD Almighty has purposed, and who can
      thwart him?
   His hand is stretched out, and who can turn it back?

(Isaiah 14:24,27)

"Remember the former things, those of long ago;
   I am God, and there is no other;
   I am God, and there is none like me.
I make known the end from the beginning,
   from ancient times, what is still to come.
I say: My purpose will stand,
   and I will do all that I please.
From the east I summon a bird of prey;
   from a far-off land, a man to fulfill my purpose.
What I have said, that will I bring about;
   what I have planned, that will I do."

(Isaiah 46:9-11)

Are you feeling more confident yet? If not, review those verses again. Say them aloud. Read them with emotion, as if you are starring in the role of your life. You are. Picture yourself on center stage acting out your dream role with God as your producer. Soon you'll be walking the red carpet toward all God has planned for you.

REACHING FOR THE STARS

As Heather Whitestone grasped her dream, she reached back to help others with theirs. Heather went to work and developed her platform, the STARS program. She wanted to help children develop a positive attitude and reach for the stars.

As she headed for the Miss Alabama contest one last time, Teresa Strickland, a friend who helped coach and encourage Heather, dropped her a note:

> Heather, stay focused on Jesus. When you're competing
> in the pageant, keep your focus on Him. If you lose your
> focus, you will not get through the tough situations. So
> follow Jesus in your heart. Don't let gossip or the audience
> or a mistake you might make control you. Only Jesus. Let
> Him rule your heart.

On the night of the contest, when the moment for the announcement of the winner arrived, Heather was on pins and needles.

> At that moment I felt a sudden sinking feeling—almost
> like a kid who has to welcome a new baby sister but feels
> that somehow she's been displaced. Then the girl next to
> me grabbed my hand...*Dear God, tell me what is going on?*
> The audience went wild. I couldn't hear the name, but
> the girl next to me turned and said, "You won. Heather,
> you won."

She couldn't hear, but she could feel the crown being pinned to her head. As she walked the stage, she waved to the crowd and gave everyone watching the "I love you" sign.

A poster of Heather wearing her crown hangs in a store in her hometown. The poster says, "They said she would only be able to get a third-grade education. Fortunately, she wasn't listening."

Take the Leap

When I was a little girl, one of my favorite hymns had the chorus, "Leaning, leaning, safe and secure from all alarms; Leaning, leaning, leaning on the everlasting arms." When we sang it, we would lean right, left, and back. I would always picture myself not just leaning but falling into the arms of my loving Father in heaven. That song reminded me of the feeling of relaxing right off the side of a swimming pool into the safe arms of a parent or my swim coach. I *knew* I would be caught. The secret of living confidently is the ability to release and let go, knowing you will be held up by God—no matter what.

A group of us who mentor young women were having lunch one day, and we were talking about the turning point in each of our lives that moved us from queasy to confident. Our stories were all similar in that each of us had an epiphany moment when we realized God really did love us and He would really "be there" for us. One mentor worded it best: "When a woman truly believes God loves her completely, thoroughly, lavishly, and unwaveringly, she will never be the same. She will have the ability to step out and risk, knowing that God and all His power and character will carry her."

I liken it to stepping into a boat. The rapids under that boat are God's strength, power, and love, moving us forward. But we have to make the decision to get into the boat. The more we take those boat rides with God, the more willing we are to get into the boat the next time. After we have ridden the rapids of the thrill of God's love, we will actually begin to crave it.

Micky is a brave friend of mine who has led several teams into war-torn countries to do ministry. She now feels compelled to carry the women of the world on her heart. She credits her confidence to her training with Youth With a Mission. Under YWAM's leadership development philosophy, young people are placed far outside their comfort zones where they have to depend on God. There they get to see Him work in miraculous ways. Micky said, "There is a phrase in YWAM: 'Once you serve God in this way, you are ruined for normal life.'"

I want to be a woman ruined for normal life. Why play it safe when I can have the thrill, the adventure, the jazz of life? When we get out of our comfort zone, when we get to the end of ourselves, that is when God shows up.

> The courage to pursue our adventure is often directly linked to whether we believe God is trustworthy.

COUNT ON IT

Courage is something we all want. Life is intimidating, and opportunities, even positive opportunities, can seem daunting and insurmountable. The courage to pursue our adventure is often directly linked to whether we believe God is trustworthy.

But how can we know God is for real? How do we know He'll be there for us when we're depending on Him? How can we know He'll keep the promises written in the Bible?

I like to go back to the first book of the Bible, to Genesis 15, my favorite chapter in the Bible. People often ask me, "Pam, why is this your favorite chapter in the Bible? How about the Beatitudes or 1 Corinthians 13—why this one?"

It is my favorite chapter because all my courage for living comes from it. You see, in Genesis 15 God promised to make Abram's offspring as many as the stars and to give him a homeland. But Abram (his name was later changed to Abraham), like all of us, wanted reassurance that God's promises would come true. So God makes a covenant with Abram. In biblical times, if someone wanted to make a covenant with another person, one of the ways they would ratify the agreement was to cut one or more animals in two and place the halves opposite each other. Then they would link their arms together and walk between the animal parts. It was their way of saying, "If I break my part of the bargain, you can do to me what we've done to these animals." A covenant was not to be taken lightly. You couldn't just hire some high-powered lawyer, find a loophole, and get out of it.

The covenant between God and Abram was a little different, though. God knew Abram was a fallible human being, incapable of keeping his part of the bargain forever. To guarantee the covenant, God put Abram to sleep and walked through the animals in the form of a smoking firepot and a blazing torch. In essence, *God made the covenant with Himself.* And since God will never die, we can be assured that

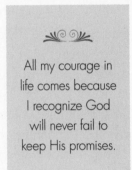

All my courage in life comes because I recognize God will never fail to keep His promises.

He will *always* keep His promises. All my courage in life comes because I recognize God will never fail to keep His promises.

Trek Forward

Often exhaustion is what moves us to the end of ourselves. When I recognize this weariness in myself, I know that only in God's presence will my courage to continue pursuing my adventure be revived.

One fall I had weeks of back-to-back speaking engagements and media appearances. On the night before a scheduled trip to Colorado, I attended my son's football game, and one of his friends he had led to Jesus was injured and had to be rushed to the hospital. My family and I went to the hospital to be with him, and at 1:00 in the morning, we were still there.

The next morning I had to wake up at 4:30 to catch my flight, and I remember thinking, *Good, my flight got booked with some breathing space. I'll get there early, take a nap, shower, and feel refreshed.* No such luck. I arrived at the Denver airport only to discover that my connecting flight had been cancelled, and I was stuck in the airport for five hours while I waited for a later flight. That meant I would have to dress for the event in an airport restroom and step off the plane and into the pulpit. My heart sank. My body longed for a bed. How was I ever going to get the rest I needed stranded in an airport?

I walked through the terminal and prayed. I spotted an empty gate and noticed the door to the outside was open, allowing fresh air to stream in. I created my own lounge chair by placing my suitcase under my legs and my purse under my head and began to read a book by A.W. Tozer about the character of God. As I read, some birds hopped into the terminal and began to feed on crumbs. I remembered the verse, "Look at the birds of the air; they do not sow or reap or store away in barns, and yet your heavenly Father feeds them. Are you not much more valuable than they?" (Matthew 6:26). I smiled, read the final page of my book, and drifted off to sweet slumber. I awoke an hour later, refreshed and thankful that those who wait on the Lord gain renewed strength and courage.

On that day, the all-knowing God created a refreshing and memorable time just for me right in the middle of a crowded and chaotic airport. Too often we panic and chase after quick-fix solutions to our stress. All the while God is waiting for us to turn to Him so He can give supernatural strength and courage to continue walking the path He has created for us.

> Find rest, O my soul, in God alone;
>   my hope comes from him.
>
>   (Psalm 62:5)

I HAVE NOTHING

It was vital I learned this, because this is the place God has kept me—at the end of my own abilities. And as I look back, this is one of the ways God keeps me accomplishing the adventures He has for me. When I am at the edge of my leadership talent, I am forced to go to His Word daily to learn how to lead at the next level. I am pressed to the edge of my education, so I have to trust God to teach me and get me into the best training programs I need for the path He sees ahead for me. I am at the edge of my available time, so I am forced to evaluate my life and prioritize the people in my world according to God's perspective, not the traditions of the past or others' expectations. I am pushed to the edge of my speaking and writing abilities, and so I am open to the critiquing, carving, and fine-tuning sent to me through God's hand (often through others). I am at the edge of my stamina, so I am forced to trust in the words of Isaiah 40, which for me often means jumping in the shower while I recite:

> Even youths grow tired and weary,
>   and young men stumble and fall;
> but those who hope in the LORD
>   will renew their strength.
> They will soar on wings like eagles;
>   they will run and not grow weary,
>   they will walk and not be faint.

(Isaiah 40:30-31)

OVER THE EDGE

The most stretching experience I had was the day the war in Iraq broke out. I had been booked two years prior to travel to Europe to speak to military wives and women on becoming "Women of Influence." Then 9/11 happened, and America found itself in a fight for survival. Also at this same time I was hit with a personal and professional blow that rocked my world, my family, and our future. I felt completely depleted by the months of trauma, and I felt an overwhelming burden for my husband and children.

In addition to this, I felt completely inadequate to be the main speaker to these amazing women. Most of them were kissing their husbands and sending them off to war. Probably some would never kiss again. These courageous women were coming to a conference on leadership, and I felt they should be leading and teaching me. I felt I had nothing to give, nothing to say as I boarded the plane for the 24-hour flight. So I simply owned my emptiness.

In prayer I cried out, *Lord, I am empty, depleted, at the end of myself. I have nothing, am nothing, know nothing. All I have is You. So, God, I am getting on this plane by faith that at the other end, when I get off, You will show up for all of us. These women deserve that, so just make me a funnel and send the best of who You are to them. Just get me out of the way.*

> Step into the boat of God's adequacy and hold on for the ride of your life.

I stretched out across the row of seats and put on my ear phones and listened to the Bible all the way across the USA and the Atlantic Ocean. God filled me up and gave me a listening heart. Within hours of landing, I could tell exactly what pieces of my messages God wanted to forge into a new set for these precious women. During the first night we cried together, the second night we laughed together, and the final night we plunged our faith stakes into the ground and proclaimed the goodness and greatness of God together. From these messages, an entire new ministry to military families was born.

Take Courage

Just admit it—you are inadequate. You will, at times, be scared to death. God knew you would be. Jesus instructed His disciples and the apostle Paul to "take courage" (Matthew 14:27; Mark 6:51; Acts 23:11). I love that picture. It's like courage is something you can pick up at the local Wal-Mart. So go—take it. God wants you to have it. To help you take courage, I've strung together a few verses that speak to that need. Just fill in your name in the blanks the next time you need a little courage:

Have I not commanded you, _____? Be
strong and courageous. Do not be terrified; do not be
discouraged, for the LORD your God will be with you
wherever you go. The LORD himself goes before you,
_____, and will be with you; he will never
leave you nor forsake you. Do not be afraid; do not be
discouraged. Rise up; this matter is in your hands. We
will support you, so take courage and do it. Be strong and
very courageous, _____. Be careful to obey
all the law my servant Moses gave you; do not turn from
it to the right or to the left, that you may be successful
wherever you go. Turn your ear to me, come quickly to my
rescue; be my rock of refuge, a strong fortress to save me.
For you have been my refuge, a strong tower against the
foe. O Sovereign LORD, my strong deliverer, who shields
my head in the day of battle. The name of the LORD is a
strong tower; the righteous run to it and are safe…for their
Defender is strong; he will take up their case against you.
Finally, _____, be strong in the Lord and in
his mighty power. Put on the full armor of God so that
you can take your stand against the devil's schemes. And
the God of all grace, who called you, _____,
to his eternal glory in Christ, after you have suffered a
little while, will himself restore you and make you strong,
firm, and steadfast…In all these things we are more than
conquerors through him who loved us.

Now take courage, and then step into the boat of God's adequacy
and hold on for the ride of your life. Let His love carry you down-
river to your dream.

DANCE INTO THE DREAM

For Heather Whitestone, the crown didn't remove all the
obstacles; it provided new ones—and new opportunities. Two
years after she was named Miss Alabama, Heather was handed a

large check in an elaborate ceremony by Elmer Harris, CEO of a public utility. It seems that an executive from his company had witnessed the following scene in an airport and had been moved to tears.

Heather had been waiting for a late airplane when she saw a woman and her daughter coming toward her. The little girl, ill and in a wheelchair, clearly recognized Heather. Seeing the girl's response, Heather took her crown out of its carrying case and placed it on the little girl's head. A small gesture. A small act of kindness that prompted the executive to tell the story to his boss.

The Heather Whitestone Foundation was launched to help others reach their adventure. Heather rested in God's character and danced into her own adventure, and now she's helping others dance into their adventure too.

Let God's winning words give you the confidence to dance into your adventure.

WINNING WORDS

When you don't feel like dancing, when you need to hurdle an obstacle, let the Lord speak to you through these verses (some of which I've paraphrased):

> God says, "I am able to do immeasurably more than all you ask or imagine, according to my power that is at work within you. Mine is the greatness and the power and the glory and the majesty and the splendor, for everything in heaven and earth is mine. Mine is the kingdom; I am exalted as head over all. Wealth and honor come from me; I am the ruler of all things. I am beyond your reach and exalted in power; in my justice and great righteousness, I do not oppress. I, the Sovereign LORD, come with power, and my arm rules for me. See, my reward is with me, and my recompense accompanies me. I give strength to the weary and increase the power of the weak. I, the Sovereign LORD, have made the heavens and the earth

by my great power and outstretched arm. Nothing is too hard for me. I rescue and save."

May the God of hope fill you with all joy and peace as you trust in him, so that you may overflow with hope by the power of the Holy Spirit.

*W*INNING WISDOM

What circumstance seems impossible in your life? Are you tired of trying? Tired of striving?

Heather Whitestone had people in her life who continually told her positive truth. Who tells you the truth about yourself and the truth about God and His strength and power? When things get really tough, ask your friends, family, or small group to tell you positive truth. Or maybe you know someone who is discouraged and feels like giving up. Bombard her life with truth: send e-mails, faxes, letters, cards, voicemail messages—all filled with positive truth.

When I come across a verse that proclaims God's awesome power, I copy it onto a brightly colored note card and post it on my bathroom mirror so I can read the verse until I have it memorized.

When we were filming a DVD Bible study for *Men Are Like Waffles, Women Are Like Spaghetti,* I struggled with the camera making me look ten pounds heavier. April, one of my mentees, gave me a precious gift of verses about how God sees me as beautiful. I put them on the mirror where I put on my makeup each day and read and reflected on them as I prepared each morning for filming. I liked the outcome so well I left them up.

*W*INNING WAYS

Have you ever needed courage and didn't know where to go? With your adventure cheerleader, read Hebrews 11, the Hall of Fame of the courageous. Each of you select one courageous soul and do a character study of that person. In your journal, answer these questions:

What obstacle was overcome?

How did he or she overcome it?

What can you glean from his or her life and apply to your own?

Now share what you learned with one another to help you hurdle your own obstacle.

If you noticed, the steps for hurdling obstacles on your way to the finish line of your adventure all began with the letter *T.* Which one of the steps will help you get back on stride toward your dream?

1. Tell the Truth

2. Take on the Adversaries

3. Trade in Your Perspective

4. Take the Leap

5. Trek Forward

6. Take Courage

God is God. He never changes and He is always reliable—every single time. Use these six steps to stay on stride toward your adventure. Let God's love ruin you for "normal life" too. The courageous race is much more exciting. Get in stride with God and run the race to your dream. The race is on, and the quest for confidence is an amazing adventure.

Risk

Face Down Failure

"The person interested in success has to
learn to view failure as a healthy, inevitable
part of the process of getting to the top."

Dr. Joyce Brothers

o ahead, embrace it, own it, acknowledge it, face it down:
you *will* fail. It's not that you might, not that you could, you
will. Every toddler when learning to walk first falls, and you
may too when you first begin to STEP into God's adventure.

Whether you're living on the edge, giving life your all, looking for the best God has for you, or just living an ordinary life,
sometime, someplace, in some way, you will fail. Most people try
to avoid the feeling of failure at all costs. But when you are afraid
of failure, you become afraid to try. And when you are afraid to try
new things, you may miss your moment because you're sitting on
the sidelines, a wallflower at your own dance party. One of the keys
to developing confidence is to embrace your failure, your past, your
humanity, and your potential mistakes.

THE DANGER OF OVERCONFIDENCE

Sometimes we encounter failure because we become overconfi-
dent. Reviewing the Bible's few descriptions of overconfidence can
be a big help. Oh, and here's a big shock—they all come from Satan!
First, check out how Satan is described before his fall:

> "You were the model of perfection,
>   full of wisdom and perfect in beauty.
> You were in Eden,
>   the garden of God;
> every precious stone adorned you…
> Your settings and mountings were made of gold;
>   on the day you were created they
>   were prepared.
> You were anointed as a guardian cherub,
>   for so I ordained you.
> You were on the holy mount of God;
>   you walked among the fiery stones.
> You were blameless in your ways
>   from the day you were created
>   till wickedness was found in you."
>
>   (Ezekiel 28:11-15)

He was a beautiful angel, perfect, made to *worship* God. Then iniquity was found in him. So what was that fatal flaw? Isaiah 14:13-14 states it simply:

> You said in your heart,
>   "I will ascend to heaven;
> I will raise my throne
>   above the stars of God;
> I will sit enthroned on the mount of assembly,
>   on the utmost heights of the sacred mountain.
> I will ascend above the tops of the clouds;
>   I will make myself like the Most High."

Satan got it in his head that *he* should become God. Satan quit serving God, he quit worshipping God, and he decided he should *be* God. This got him booted out.

> But you are brought down to the grave,
>   to the depths of the pit.
>
>   (Isaiah 14:15)

Strike one: *Pride* leads to overconfidence—thinking you are better, smarter, more capable than God.

Then we see Satan in the Garden of Eden. There is Eve, minding her own business, tending the perfect garden God prepared for her, living with a perfect man (can you imagine?) and enjoying a perfectly stress-free life. Then along comes the serpent and tempts her. She knew the tree of life was out of bounds. God required that she obey only one command, "You must not eat from the tree of the knowledge of good and evil." Well, Satan convinced her he had a better idea than God's. And *bam*—life has never been the same. (Eve, I'm going to "thank you" for PMS and menopause when I get to heaven!)

Strike two: *Presumption* leads to overconfidence—thinking you have a better plan than God's.

You would think Satan would learn, but no, he even tries to tempt Jesus:

> Then Jesus was led by the Spirit into the desert to be tempted by the devil. After fasting forty days and forty nights, he was hungry. The tempter came to him and said, "If you are the Son of God, tell these stones to become bread."
>
> Jesus answered, "It is written: 'Man does not live on bread alone, but on every word that comes from the mouth of God.'"
>
> Then the devil took him to the holy city and had him stand on the highest point of the temple. "If you are the Son of God," he said, "throw yourself down. For it is written:
>
> "'He will command his angels concerning you,
> and they will lift you up in their hands,
> so that you will not strike your foot
> against a stone.'"
>
> Jesus answered him, "It is also written: 'Do not put the Lord your God to the test'" (Matthew 4:1-7).

Notice how Jesus handles Satan's contentions. Jesus fasted, and then He factually answered with the truth. If you're wondering whether it's a promise or a presumption that you're claiming God will do, fast first. Then research several Bible verses on that subject so you get the "whole counsel of God." A promise of God in Scripture is bedrock; a presumption is a self-proclaimed, reckless, sinking sandpit. Check where you're standing.

Strike three: *Pleasure* leads to overconfidence—thinking the world (and God) revolves around you and exists for your pleasure. If you get yourself in a jam, you think God owes it to you to come to your rescue. Satan tried that on Jesus too:

> Again, the devil took him to a very high mountain and showed him all the kingdoms of the world and their splendor. "All this I will give you," he said, "if you will bow down and worship me."
>
> Jesus said to him, "Away from me, Satan! For it is written: 'Worship the Lord your God, and serve him only.'"
>
> Then the devil left him, and angels came and attended him (Matthew 4:8-11).

Notice Jesus put Satan in his rightful place—off the throne of self-indulgence. God doesn't exist for our pleasure; we exist for His. Pride, presumption, and pleasure—watch out for these as they feed the monster of overconfidence lying dormant in every soul.

CONFIDENCE VS. OVERCONFIDENCE

Two days stand out in my mind as reminders of the complications of overconfidence. The first day began benignly. It was a Friday, and I was traveling—just two flights with a simple connection in San Francisco—to Central Oregon to speak that evening.

I got to the airport early, before breakfast, and discovered that the San Francisco airport was fogged in, planes were backed up, and flights were delayed. Everything was being rerouted. They readjusted my tickets to route me through Los Angeles, and when

I landed there, I checked my messages because the airline said my travel agent would rebook my second leg from LAX. My agent had placed me on a flight that arrived in Redmond, Oregon, at 10:00 p.m., but I was supposed to speak at 7:00. I made my way to the ticket agent and explained my plight.

On days like this, any seat is hard to come by, but while I was speaking, the agent said, "Wow! A miracle! One ticket on the earlier flight just appeared, but it leaves in just a couple minutes so you need to rush to Gate 20."

I arrived at Gate 20 out of breath and saw the sign over the doorway that read *Redmond, OR.* The announcement was made for final boarding, and I handed the gate agent my boarding pass. I followed the crowd through the doorway and into the rain, only to see 15 identical planes in a semicircle. I followed the crowd and boarded a plane, sat in seat 2A, and pulled out my books. A woman entered and said she also was assigned 2A, but then she simply took another seat. We prepared for takeoff, and because I can repeat from memory the "mask-dropping-in-case-of-loss-of-cabin-pressure" flight instructions, I tuned out the flight attendant. I lost myself in my work for approximately an hour, until we landed and the flight attendant said, "Welcome to Santa Barbara."

"What! What did you say?" I exclaimed.

"Welcome to Santa Barbara."

"But I'm supposed to be in Redmond, Oregon, right now!"

As soon as I got off the plane, I called the meeting planner. But what exactly do you say to someone you've never met, who has entrusted you with the women under her care because of your "wisdom," and you just overconfidently got on the wrong plane going the wrong way?

When I got my patient, precious planner on the phone, she simply said, "Where are you?"

"I will explain more when I arrive, but that won't be until 10 p.m. So can I give you some discussion questions for the women to use in preparation for the topic I'll start with tomorrow?"

She obliged. I reboarded the plane and flew back to LAX, back to the same gate with "Redmond, OR" written over it.

This time, however, things were much different. The announcer belted out, "Redmond, Oregon." The gate agent looked me in the eye and said, "Redmond, Oregon?" and then ran my boarding pass through the electronic reader. I stepped into the doorway, and an agent with a sign that read "Redmond" walked us to the correct plane. As I boarded this time, the attendant asked, "Redmond, Oregon?" I nodded. And I heard every word of the preflight instructions, including a welcome to the plane traveling to Redmond.

> Sometimes the most dangerous place is the comfort zone of our past successes because we begin to live by presumption rather than reliance on God's power.

On the plane I pondered my blunder. How could someone who travels every week get on the wrong plane? Sure, I could blame the airlines, but I knew I was at least as much to blame. I had missed vital information due to my overconfidence. You better believe that when I board a plane now, I ask where it's going!

Sometimes the most dangerous place is the comfort zone of our past successes because we begin to live by presumption rather than reliance on God's power. Pay attention to the routine of the dream and keep yourself plugged into the details. Building a track record is good, and success builds up your confidence, but presuming without putting in the time or attention is the slippery slope to failure.

RECORD-BREAKING OVERCONFIDENCE

The other day that helps me remember what overconfidence looks like is the day I got two speeding tickets on two separate coasts—three times zones apart. And on Mother's Day no less!

I think I deserve a place in *Guinness World Records*.

The first ticket was really not my fault. Honest! Early Mother's

Day morning in Virginia, I drove with my two younger sons to join my eldest and his wife at their church. I pulled out of the hotel and headed to our destination. Almost as soon as I got on the four-lane thoroughfare, I heard the siren and saw the lights in my rearview mirror. I had no idea why I was being pulled over. I was traveling the same speed as I would on a similar road in California. Unfortunately for me, the posting of the speed limit was several hundred feet ahead of me, just out of sight. However, I quickly discovered that making the excuse that I didn't know about and couldn't possibly see the posting that far ahead (or even whining it was Mother's Day) made no impression on the officer.

Ticket number one was the result of a basic human error; we're all imperfect. However, ticket number two...now that's a different story.

After church and after lunch with my wonderful children, I drove four hours in the pouring rain to Washington's Dulles airport, arriving two hours before my flight. When I walked in, I realized that two hours might not be enough to navigate the longest check-in line in airline history. I barely made my flight to Portland but my luggage did not. It was midnight. A sane woman would have said, "I need to get a hotel room and not attempt the three-hour drive on back roads to the Oregon coast. I should wait until morning."

But I was not sane. I was zealous. I thought, *I am known for being intense, so intense I will be.* (Strike one: *Pride.*)

I had a meeting the next day and didn't want to reschedule it. I wanted to get to the coast, have the meeting, and then start on the "deeply spiritual book-writing week" I had planned. I'd just get some food, some panties and pj's, look for some good coffee, and I'd be good to go, right?

Wrong. So completely wrong.

I made it to a 24-hour grocery store but then promptly got lost. I had to call my husband and wake him out of a dead sleep to help me get back to the freeway and locate the correct exit.

"Are you sure you want to drive?" he sleepily said. "Don't you want to get a hotel room?"

I pulled out my Superwoman cape and persuaded my almost comatose husband I'd be fine. (*Besides, the condo on the coast is free. Why pay for a hotel?* I reasoned with heroic bravado.)

"Are you sure?" Bill said. "Hey, our friends Frank and Kendyl are just a few miles from where you are. Want me to call them and see if you can stay there?"

"It's after midnight. It's too late to just drop by. Honey, really, I'm fine. MapQuest says I'm almost there. Really, I'll be fine."

"You're a big girl; you decide. But please feel free to get a hotel if you get tired along the way. I want you back in one piece. I love you."

Oh yeah, I was working my plan, even if it killed me! (Strike two: *Presumption.*)

I turned up the radio and sang to a golden oldies station, cranked up the air conditioning, sipped my latte, and pretended I was Dianna Ross on a road trip. I was traveling diva style, my way on the highway.

Well, I was bebopping along, all full of myself with a kind of Aretha Franklin "R-E-S-P-E-C-T," Helen Reddy "I am woman, hear me roar," with a little Shania Twain "feel like a woman," invincible attitude. Oh yeah, I was Supergirl, and I was flying now.

Well, driving on the back roads to the Oregon coast proved much more perilous than MapQuest described. The roads were pitch black, and I was all alone on them. The speed limit signs seemed to change every 40 feet, and I was always adjusting my speed from 50 to 30 to 25 to 40.

Somewhere along the way I must have missed a speed limit sign because the next thing I knew, I heard the familiar siren and saw the all-too-familiar flashing lights. The officer asked if I had been drinking. I assured him I had not because my father was an alcoholic and I had sworn off booze. Well, my confession got no sympathy.

Then he asked me what I had been doing that day. I asked, "You want to know what I've done all day?" He assured me he did, and so I gave him a minute-by-minute rundown of my whereabouts since rising at 5:30 a.m. Eastern time (it was now 2 a.m. Pacific).

"That's a long day," he said.

And then I added in my other woes—lost bags, getting lost in Portland, feeling afraid on the dark back roads (I left out getting the ticket in Virginia). He was slightly moved, so I said, "And it's Mother's Day and I'm a mom." I thought the tears over the lost bags and it being Mother's Day were nice touches. I was hoping it was going to get me off. I thought, *I mean, really, can't he see that I'm a busy woman carrying a mountain of responsibility, and I need a week at the beach? I deserve a week at the beach. I have earned a week at the beach!*

> The opposite of overconfidence, or confidence in our own power, is to be confident in God's power.

With a genuine look of concern on his face, he handed me the ticket. (Strike three: *Pleasure.*)

Still, I forged ahead. This time I carefully obeyed the speed limit and finally made it to the hotel (after getting lost yet once more). I arrived in one piece and fell into bed as the sun rose. I awoke several hours later and checked the time. *11:00 A.M.* The sun beaming in the window must have awakened me.

> *Lord, that's the last time I'm going to don my Wonder Woman cape. I'm too old for these all-nighters. I also can't afford them. Two tickets in one day—I could have stayed at a five-star hotel for the week for what I will pay in fines. Plus I could have died, or the car could have broken down on some desolate road without cell coverage. Who knows who would have stopped by—a Good Samaritan or Jack the Ripper! Lord, I am sorry. I'm turning in my superhero cape. No more crazy all-nighters. Thanks for saving my life.*

THE BLESSING OF BROKENNESS

Laurence J. Peter, author of *The Peter Principle: Why Things Always Go Wrong,* says there are two kinds of failures: those who thought and never did, and those who did and never thought.[1]

The opposite of overconfidence, or confidence in our own power, is to be confident in God's power. If we place our lives in God's hands, He promises to be with us when we encounter situations that involve great risk. Debra Maffett, crowned Miss America in 1983, has experienced God's faithfulness in her life on more than one occasion.[2]

Debra had run for Miss Texas three times when a friend convinced her to come to California for a spot on a television show. After she arrived, the Miss California people encouraged her to compete in their pageant.

> I had risked everything to come out to California. I had $300 to my name, and I knew if I didn't win the pageant, I couldn't get home. My parents didn't have the money to get me home. I had worked in a bakery to put myself through college and to pay for five years of pageants and voice lessons. I had gathered sponsors to help out along the way, and it really was blood, sweat, and tears to get me to the pageant each time. But I borrowed $1,500 to get me through three months of living expenses and packed everything in my little beat-up car to get to Santa Cruz where the pageant was held.

At the pageant, Debra was chosen as one of the ten finalists, but she felt she had completely blown the talent portion.

> I felt that not only had I lost, I had lost embarrassingly. The orchestra leader had to signal the orchestra to stop. I wanted a crack in the stage to open up and the stage to swallow me. I wondered if they would let me start over for a moment, but I knew they wouldn't so I finished the song a cappella, and I walked off the stage devastated. I could even hear some of the girls backstage cheering because I had blown it.

One godly older woman working backstage pulled Debra aside, offered up a quick prayer, and said, "It's not over till it's over. You walk out there with your chin held high."

When the final contestants were called onto the stage for the naming of the winner, Debra was barely holding on to her composure.

> I was getting ready to lose it bad. I felt I was going to cry hard, so hard that it would have been embarrassing. I kept thinking about all those years of hard work, that because of my age, this was my last shot, that if I lost I had nowhere to go, nowhere to live, no money to return home. I thought about how I had lived my life, how I focused on my goals, my dreams. I had never stopped to ask God if these were His dreams for my life. At that moment I told God I was sorry, sorry I hadn't done life God's way.
>
> Then I realized those five years weren't wasted. I had learned so much. I prayed, *God, I didn't think of what You wanted, what You had for me. God, if You will just give me the strength to walk off this stage without losing it emotionally, I will be Yours. I will go where You want me to go, do what You want me to do, be who You want me to be.*
>
> I think that was the first time I had ever really cried out to God. Instantly, I was flooded with peace. It was so awesome, so welcome. It no longer mattered to me if I won. I knew at that moment that God would watch over me and give me peace.
>
> Then they called out my name as Miss California. I cried for three straight days.

Debra had just a few short months to prepare for the Miss America pageant, and she was dreading the talent portion, even though she had heard that her stumble during her Miss California pageant performance had been edited out of the tape. "I knew that same horrible fear that had caused me to blow my talent over and over was still there. I knew the fear hadn't been edited out." To make matters worse, the news of Debra's weakness traveled the pageant grapevine. Debra bolstered her courage by seeking out God.

> Some precious prayer warriors involved in the California pageant took me to a little church and prayed over me. I started getting into God's Word and used it for prayer. I also got to talk to a former Miss America who had an inner strength, beauty, and confidence, and I asked her how she handled the talent section. She replied, "When I get up on stage, I pray that God would use me as a vessel to pour His love out to the audience." I realized then that my focus had been all wrong.

The day of the pageant arrived, and when it was time for Debra to perform, she was petrified.

> I cried out to God, *Please let me pour out Your love.* I felt His presence so strong. I had so much peace, I had no fear. It was like I had been scooped up and set in a special quiet place. After I performed, I knew I had performed better than I ever had, and I knew I had supernatural help. I knew it didn't matter if I won. I had learned all I needed to learn. No matter what I had to face in life, I could turn to God and completely lean on His strength and ability, and I could make it through anything.

Sometimes we encounter failure because we make poor choices.

Debra was crowned Miss America. "I learned to embrace trial and learned to praise God in the valley, because when you're there, God pulls back the veil and you get a bigger picture. When we lean on our strength, we cut off God's power, but when we enter into His rest and cling to Christ, all of who He is can flow through us."

WHEN IT ALL UNRAVELS

Sometimes we encounter failure because we make poor choices. Her name was in the headlines daily, her photo plastered in every newspaper and on the cover of nearly every magazine. Her name was a household word. Every tabloid maliciously labeled her: Donna Rice, the vixen who sidetracked Gary Hart's bid for the presidency.

How could a nice Christian girl, raised in a conservative church-going family, end up so off track?

After graduating from college in 1980, Donna ended up in New York City to try to launch her acting career, but she soon decided to move to Miami where she began a successful career as a television commercial actress.

One night while with friends, Donna met Senator Gary Hart at a fund-raiser. The party was so crowded that a small group, including Donna, went outside and on to a yacht owned by the resort's owner. After boarding, the group discovered that the boat was chartered by Senator Hart and some of his friends. Realizing their mistake, the group apologized and turned to leave—but they were invited to stay. As Donna was leaving the yacht later that night, Senator Hart asked for her phone number, and the next day, she and a friend were invited out for an afternoon on the ocean.

> Gary was the one who swept me off my feet. Before the boat docked, however, he confessed that because he was contemplating running for president, he couldn't separate from his wife. I believed him when he told me he faced a difficult choice between pursuing personal happiness and his political destiny.
>
> After he left Miami, he called me regularly. Two weeks later, he announced in a press conference he was running for president. When Gary continued to call, I became confused about his true feelings for me—and my own.
>
> One night, I flipped on the television and began watching the movie *Jesus of Nazareth*. Suddenly I was struck

with how far off course I'd gotten, and I knew I couldn't continue with my current lifestyle. So on May 1, 1987, at Gary's invitation, I agreed to see him one last time—to confront him face to face about his sincerity and with the intention of ending our brief relationship. I didn't know I was walking into a trap—that reporters had been tipped off to stake out his house.[3]

Months later, during a *20/20* interview, Donna finally put the pieces together. A friend of Donna's had taken pictures of Donna and Gary aboard ship. The "friend" had tried to sell the photos to the press, but the press demanded a story. Donna was set up so that events could unfold before the watchful eyes of the press who wanted to get a story about Senator Hart, the "womanizer." Soon Donna saw photos of herself plastered in the tabloids. She was shocked and devastated to find herself center stage in the scandal of the presidential political election. She felt trapped and hopeless.

SAME SONG, SECOND VERSE

Roll the hands of time back, and history provides abundant examples of women with destroyed reputations. Rahab was such a woman. People mocked her, whispered behind her back, laughed—but the men kept coming back. She was very good at what she did, and her family depended on her to provide—even if it was through prostitution.

One day some strangers came to town, and like many out-of-towners, they ended up at her house. But these men were different. They didn't want to use her. They extended a compassionate glance, a kind word, and instead of bringing pain they brought peace. Even though these men were spies, Rahab agreed to hide them in her home, and she boldly asked them to protect her family when the Israelites marched against Jericho:

> Before the spies lay down for the night, she went up on the roof and said to them, "I know that the LORD has given

this land to you and that a great fear of you has fallen on us, so that all who live in this country are melting in fear because of you…Now then, please swear to me by the LORD that you will show kindness to my family, because I have shown kindness to you. Give me a sure sign that you will spare the lives of my father and mother, my brothers and sisters, and all who belong to them, and that you will save us from death"…

"Our lives for your lives!" the men assured her. "If you don't tell what we are doing, we will treat you kindly and faithfully when the LORD gives us the land."

The men said to her, "This oath you made us swear will not be binding on us unless, when we enter the land, you have tied this scarlet cord in the window through which you let us down…But if you tell what we are doing, we will be released from the oath you made us swear."

"Agreed," she replied. "Let it be as you say." So she sent them away and they departed. And she tied the scarlet cord in the window (Joshua 2:8-21).

Days later, Rahab saw the Israelites marching toward Jericho. She might have thought, *Can this God of theirs really be trusted? Is He just like the men I know—will He just use me and toss me aside too? Or is He really as strong and powerful—and good—as I've heard in the rumors and from the lips of the Israelite spies?* Then she remembered the peace, the hope, the respect she had felt when the Israelite men came to her home. She wanted that hope every day for herself and her family, so she hung the scarlet cord out the window, praying, *God, please be who they say You are.*

Then the troops began to march. Day after day they marched. Finally, on the seventh day they drew their trumpets and the music blared—and the wall around Jericho fell, except for the place where the scarlet cord hung out the window. God was faithful, even to a hurting prostitute wishing for a fresh start.

GO BACK, MOVE FORWARD

Donna Rice wished for a fresh start as well. The media feeding frenzy just worsened. She had to leave her job, and she couldn't stay anywhere longer than a week before the press found her. She wondered if she should speak out or keep silent as lies and half-truths were paraded before the public. She had no private life anymore. She had become the bimbo poster girl. Like the walls of Jericho, her world seemed to be crumbling around her.

How did Donna pick herself up and go on when life seemed to just be headed for more and more pain? She called home, and she called out to God for mercy. Rahab cried out, Donna cried out, and all women looking for confidence cry out: *Please be who I know Your Word says You are.*

If your fists are closed around the past, they are not open to receive the new thing God wants to give you.

God answered her cry for mercy and surrounded her with His love. Donna went to church and sobbed through the services. Her mother mailed her an audiotape from an old youth group friend that said, "Donna, I imagine you're in a lot of pain right now. I just want you to know God loves you and I love you." Christian friends formed a protective circle around her and helped her sort through phone calls, media offers, and book deals. She found a new Christian roommate. At a prayer breakfast in Washington, D.C., she met some Christians who offered her a retreat, and for the next few months she rested there and gained renewed strength.

After the retreat, May Doremus, a leader of the prayer breakfast, offered Donna a safe place to stay in her home with her husband and two children. Donna humbly accepted. At the time, May was confined to a wheelchair and was a medical enigma. Donna felt like a social enigma, so the bond of friendship grew, as did Donna's relationship with God.

SEEDS OF RENEWAL

Bernadette Devlin said, "To gain that which is worth having, it may be necessary to lose everything else." Sometimes to move forward, we have to be willing to let go of the past. My friend Teresa shared this bit of wisdom with me while on a walk during a difficult time in my life: "If your fists are closed around the past, they are not open to receive the new thing God wants to give you."

> When you feel you're at the end of a road, go back to the promises that have helped you know God's will in the past and pray them today.

During the most difficult crisis and what seemed like a failure in my own life, I wrote this devotional to my prayer team and sent it with a packet of flower seeds:

> "I tell you the truth, unless a kernel of wheat falls to the ground and dies, it remains only a single seed. But if it dies, it produces many seeds" (John 12:24).

One day I was sitting in a friend's church worshipping. We were at her church because my husband had a health issue that made it impossible to continue leading both the church ministry and our parachurch writing and speaking ministry. We had just completed a nice new building for our own congregation, 15 years of work, sacrifice, and love went into those walls and more so into those people. We had hoped to transition to another part-time role at the church and also full-time minister through our writing and speaking, but in the end that was not the plan that worked out. I sat in my friend's church, broken. During a worship song, I prayed.

God, Bill is such a good man. Such a godly man. Such a great teacher and shepherd. This is just so hard. Bill preached on the life of Moses to move the church from temporary facilities through the building project and into our promised land. But like Moses, we didn't get to go into the promised land. And Lord, it feels like David, who gathered all the goods for the temple, but Solomon built the temple. God it feels like Stephen, a good man who was stoned so early in the book of Acts, he never saw the church and its power.

Then the Holy Spirit seemed to whisper to me, "Moses, David, Stephen. Seems like pretty good company. Seems like the kind of people you have always prayed I'd make you two." Moses, a patriarch of Israel, prepared specifically by God to move his treasured people into freedom; David, a man after God's own heart, often seen as Israel's greatest king; Stephen, the first martyr.

Then I was reminded of the verse, "unless a seed falls to the ground and dies…" *Dies.* Lord, this does feel like death, death of a dream. "But if it dies, it produces many seeds," the Spirit reminded. In my mind, I took the dream of the ministry I thought we'd have, placed it in the ground, like a seed, and prayed, "God give me the new harvest, the new fruit You have for us."

May God bless each of you, our friends. Bill and I feel we are in "good company" with each of you. We may all be fellowshipping with many congregations, under different walls and roofs, but we know God will be faithful to you and your character and your work and sacrifice. We are praying new, glorious, amazing fruit for each of you, for your families, in your ministries, and as we all are teamed up as Friends of Masterful Living, may we see God give great lasting fruit through Masterful Living.

We love and value *you*,
Pam and Bill

God is not unjust; he will not forget your work and the love you have shown him as you have helped his people and continue to help them (Hebrews 6:10).

When you feel you're at the end of a road, go back. Go back to the place where you know you've heard God's voice before. Go back to the people who have helped you discover God's will in the past. Go back to the promises that have helped you know God's will in the past and pray them today. In going back, many times you gain the wisdom and strength to move forward.

God walked Donna back through her life. In college she'd drifted and compromised her Christian values. She drank, partied, and dated non-Christians. After graduation she dated an older guy, and one night after a few drinks, he forced her to have sex. Her virginity taken by a date rape, Donna felt afraid, ashamed, and unloved.

The rape left her feeling like used goods, and she soon began a spiral downward into promiscuity even as her acting and modeling career took her upward into glitzy social circles. It was at this time of inner turmoil that she met Gary Hart, and her life fell apart.

Sorting through these old wounds, extending forgiveness to all those who had used her, and accepting God's forgiveness for herself launched Donna forward again. Over the next few years, she climbed out of her depression. She began to read the Bible regularly, attend church, and listen to Christian radio. She surrounded herself with friends who wanted the best for her and would hold her accountable if she felt tempted to stray. Donna says:

> God longs to rescue us out of our trouble even if we brought on the calamity by our actions and decisions.

> There are no easy answers, no quick solutions. But God is the great Restorer. In my case, I learned that although God loves us, He doesn't grant us immunity from the consequences of our choices. However, when we mess up, if we ask His forgiveness, He'll redeem those choices, using our mistakes as a "door of hope" for other people (Hosea 2:14-15).

THE DOOR OF HOPE

God longs to rescue us out of our trouble even if we brought on the calamity by our actions and decisions. He is able to restore us and redeem us if we own up to our sin and ask for mercy. When we leave our bargaining chips out of the deal and come to Him, ready to leave our rebellious ways behind and seek His righteousness, we will find that God is full of mercy. All through the Bible we see evidence of this truth:

- The sacrifices of God are a broken spirit; a broken and contrite heart, O God, you will not despise (Psalm 51:17).

- Let the wicked forsake his way and the evil man his thoughts. Let him turn to the LORD, and he will have mercy on him, and to our God, for he will freely pardon (Isaiah 55:7).

- Blessed are the merciful, for they will be shown mercy (Matthew 5:7).

- Therefore, I urge you, brothers, in view of God's mercy, to offer your bodies as living sacrifices, holy and pleasing to God—this is your spiritual act of worship (Romans 12:1).

- But for that very reason I was shown mercy so that in me, the worst of sinners, Christ Jesus might display his unlimited patience as an example for those who would believe on him and receive eternal life (1 Timothy 1:16).

Are you disappointed in the person you see in the mirror each morning? When people talk about integrity and accountability, are you squeamish, afraid of being found out? Have you made some poor choices, lapsed in your judgment, and are now waiting for the other shoe to drop? Don't wait for the other shoe to drop—run to God now and confess it all to Jesus. His mercy is freeing, His grace restoring. His death on the cross is your door of hope.

Donna walked through that door of hope and discovered that she could use her experiences to help others find God's mercy and peace by working with the Enough Is Enough campaign, an organization that fights pornography.

"Because of my experiences, I have great empathy for victims of sexual abuse and pornography," Donna says. "Through Enough Is Enough, God is using what I've learned to impact other's lives and bring Him glory. He's brought purpose to my pain—and He's thrown in some surprises too, including my husband, Jack!"

Donna married Jack in 1994, and now she's a mother, a wife, and a successful advocate for God's standards.

The door of hope is open for you too. Step across God's threshold from failure to mercy.

WINNING WORDS

The words below have been prayed over mistakes small and large, from courtrooms and prison cells to corporate offices and classrooms. We all make mistakes. Every day I plead the mercy of Jesus over my life. Join me under the waterfall of God's forgiveness:

O Lord, have mercy on me; heal me, for I have sinned against you. I am in deep distress. Let me fall into the hands of the Lord, for his mercy is great; but do not let me fall into the hands of men. In your great mercy you did not put an end to me or abandon me, for you are a gracious and merciful God. Remember me for this also, O my God, and show mercy to me according to your great love. Though I were innocent, I could not answer him; I could only plead with my Judge for mercy. In my alarm I said, "I am cut off from your sight!" Yet you heard my cry for mercy when I called to you for help. Do not withhold your mercy from me, O Lord; may your love and your truth always protect me. Have mercy on me, O God, according to your unfailing love; according to your great compassion blot out my transgressions. Have mercy on me, O God, have mercy on me, for in you my soul takes refuge. I will take refuge in the shadow of your wings until the disaster has passed. May your mercy come quickly to meet me, for I am in desperate need.

Who is a God like you, who pardons sin and forgives the transgression of the remnant of his inheritance? You do not stay angry forever but delight to show mercy. Your mercy extends to those who fear you, from generation to generation. The wisdom that comes from heaven is first of all pure; then peace-loving, considerate, submissive, full of mercy and good fruit, impartial and sincere. Let us then approach the throne of grace with confidence, so that we may receive mercy and find grace to help us in our time of need. Praise be to the God and Father of our Lord Jesus Christ! In his great mercy he has given us new birth into a living hope through the resurrection of Jesus Christ from the dead. Mercy triumphs over judgment!

WINNING WISDOM

Have you ever had to face up to a failure, the shame of poor decisions, or the humiliation of shortsighted thinking? To whom did you turn to pour out your feelings of embarrassment and disgrace? Where did you go to feel safe enough to start again?

God wants to extend mercy to us when we fail. He has set a process in place to move us from a broken place to a better place.

Acknowledge God as the giver of grace. "And the LORD said, 'I will cause all my goodness to pass in front of you, and I will proclaim my name, the LORD, in your presence. I will have mercy on whom I will have mercy, and I will have compassion on whom I will have compassion'" (Exodus 33:19).

Acknowledge your sin (the mistake, the wrong choice, rebellious act or attitude). "He who conceals his sins does not prosper, but whoever confesses and renounces them finds mercy" (Proverbs 28:13). Don't make excuses or rationalize—confess.

Amend your mistakes as much as possible. If you hurt another, apologize. If you can correct the mistake, then do so. If you can make amends, try to restore the relationship. You may find new allies as you seek to make amends. To build a new life after a failure, you'll need a new support network to help you build new habits to replace old destructive ones. Replace old destructive thoughts and patterns by renewing your mind. Start with meditating and memorizing the winning words in this chapter.

Actively pursue accountability. Sin sneaks in. Begin to pray about who you would like to have as your "fine-tuning friends." Read and discuss this book together to lay a foundation for your friendship. Look at your schedules and create a weekly time for this level of friendship—a space for a walk, lunch, coffee, or prayer.

Advance in a forward plan. Pray and ask God whether you should stay put or restart somewhere else. At times, the sin might have so negatively affected people you love that it is time to "get out of the graveyard." Luke 9:62 gives God's advice: "But Jesus said to him, 'No one, after putting his hand to the plow and looking back, is fit for the kingdom of God'" (NASB). When people see you, if all they think of is the sin, the death of the dream caused by your actions, it may be time to start over elsewhere.

Sometimes God does ask you to stay and make amends and rebuild among the ruins. He allowed David to stay in leadership after his sin with Bathsheba, but he had to endure the humiliation of his own son Absalom's attempt to usurp the throne. There may be ramifications and consequences, sometimes severe ones, if God commands you to stay put and rebuild. Don't expect others to just forgive and forget. You will have to earn the right to lead. You are not starting from zero in your attempt to build credibility. You are starting with a deficit, so be very patient with people as they learn to trust you again.

Winning Ways

Make a commitment to be totally honest in your group of fine-tuning friends. Share one failure you have experienced and what you learned from that experience. If you are struggling with a past mistake and how to regroup from it and regain your momentum, ask your friends to be your sounding board and give you ideas on ways to restart life.

I begin each day praying God's grace and mercy over my life. Before I even get out of bed, I acknowledge my humanity and propensity for mistakes and failure. Grace is God giving us what we do not deserve; mercy is God *not* giving us what we do deserve (eternal punishment).

Pray the mercy verses over each other in your group, and then thank God for His amazing grace.

STEP into God's Adventure

Speak the Adventure
Team up for the Adventure
Energize the Adventure
Push the Adventure

Protect the Adventure

A Winning Team

> "Women are the real architects of society."
>
> HARRIET BEECHER STOWE

I think some of the best orators I've ever heard are African-American pastors. Martin Luther King Jr's "I Have a Dream" is a masterpiece. I especially love these lines:

[E]ven though we face the difficulties of today and tomorrow, I still have a dream. It is a dream deeply rooted in the American dream.

I have a dream that one day this nation will rise up and live out the true meaning of its creed, "We hold these truths to be self-evident: that all men are created equal."

I have a dream that one day on the red hills of Georgia the sons of former slaves and the sons of former slave owners will be able to sit down together at the table of brotherhood.

I have a dream that one day even the state of Mississippi, a state sweltering with the heat of injustice, sweltering with the heat of oppression, will be transformed into an oasis of freedom and justice.

I have a dream that my four little children will one day

live in a nation where they will not be judged by the color
of their skin but by the content of their character.
I have a *dream* today.[1]

Notice the repeating theme, the verbal imagery, the strength
of conviction these words depict. They are powerful, life-giving
words.

THE HEART OF THE ADVENTURE

A person with heart protects and empowers her team.

When it comes to protecting and
motivating your adventure team, use
powerful, life-giving words. I'm pretty
sure you'd like your team to use those
same kind of words when sending messages your direction. The words above are
well penned, but the power is between
the lines: passion. Dr. King had the heart to lead millions through
one of the most difficult, turbulent times in our history. A person
with heart protects and empowers her team.

In a *Time* magazine interview with 90-year-old Nelson Mandela, the leader who broke the back of apartheid in South Africa
and then went on to lead that country, he gives his rules of leadership and influence. The first rule is: "Courage is not the absence of
fear—it is inspiring others to move beyond it."[2]

Your team, those closest to you, is looking to your words for
inspiration and your heart for leadership and protection. Your heart
condition protects your team, but it also protects your dream.

You are most likely one of those women who is looking for an
adventure that will make you feel alive and give your loved ones suf-
ficient resources to make their lives worthwhile as well. The power
to walk in the adventure comes from your heart. When your heart
is soft toward the Lord and invested in His adventure for your life,
you will be amazed at how much energy, focus, and determination
you can put into the adventure. God actually commits Himself to

the adventure when your heart is in the right place. "For the eyes of the LORD range throughout the earth to strengthen those whose hearts are fully committed to him" (2 Chronicles 16:9).

DYNAMITE: THE POWER BEHIND THE ADVENTURE

While traveling as a child, I watched a tunnel being built through a mountain. The dynamite used to create that tunnel for a new highway was a powerful force for good. In more recent times, we have seen the negative impact of the power of dynamite in the hands of terrorists.

The condition of your heart can be the passion that propels your dream forward, but it can also be the force that destroys your adventure before it ever reaches its potential.

Three contributors to the condition of our hearts help determine whether we are advancing the adventure or draining it of its vitality. The first is *holiness*, a commitment on your part to consistently seek God and return to His ways when you sense your heart is drifting. The second is *humility*, a commitment to live according to God's design for you. The third is your *huddle*, those close family members you naturally value most and who make the adventure worth living.

HOLINESS

A commitment to holiness is one of the most powerful elements to your dream. Holiness is not an attempt to be perfect on earth. Rather, it is a decision to manage the paradox of your heart. In your heart you desire to serve God and honor Him with your life. At the same time, you

Holiness is a lot like walking a steep mountain trail. If you keep to the sure-footed path, it will lead you to the heights.

desire to be selfish, self-centered, and self-fulfilled at any cost. All of us face this struggle, and the struggle is intense. Your ability and willingness to manage the battle that rages inside you will determine whether the dream can become a reality or if it will get lost in the distractions of your heart.

Holiness is a lot like walking a steep mountain trail. If you keep to the sure-footed path, it will lead you to the heights; if you veer from that path, a sheer cliff will lead to your demise. The goal is to stay on the sure-footed path.

LaNette was a talented actress married to a wonderful, godly, supportive man. He paid for classes so she could complete a degree. He footed the bill for supplies and all the legal paperwork for her to launch a successful business, yet she was not satisfied. Nothing seemed to ever be enough for her, and eventually she left her kind, successful, good looking husband (did I mention he was a great dad too?). She left this great guy for a man who she thought would give her more passion, excitement, and attention.

Let's get this clear: LaNette was *not* chasing God's dream. She was running from the brokenness of her past. She might have been running to try to find the dad she never knew growing up, or running to find herself, or running to fill some emptiness in her heart that only God can fill. But she was not running in God's plan.

If you have to abandon a good husband or your children or healthy moral standards to pursue the adventure, it is not God's adventure!

Zoey was a beautiful woman. She looked years younger than the 45 on her driver's license. One reason she looked younger is that she behaved younger. She dressed provocatively, much more so than her three teen daughters. She began to ditch her stable, godly husband to go "clubbing," and a man at the club talked her into working there. She told her husband she was following her midlife dream, but soon her dream turned into a nightmare with DUI charges, drug-possession charges, and an affair. Her daughters became confused and rebellious. Finally, her exhausted and brokenhearted husband left.

Zoey wasn't chasing God's dream but a dream of her own making. She still lives in her own reality far from the blessings in the real world God had (and still has) in store for her if she'd only run to Him instead of the bottle or the arms of men.

Both these women, just like hundreds of others I have talked to on the trail to self-destruction, started off crediting God with their insatiable pursuit of the adventure. But if you have to abandon a good husband or your children or healthy moral standards to pursue the adventure, it is not God's adventure! The Bible tells us Satan can disguise himself as an angel of light, and he comes to steal, kill, and destroy. If the adventure looks good but is destroying your morals, recheck the source of that adventure.

My friend, author Julie Barnhill, always prays, "Deeper in and higher up." Our job is to press deeper in so God can lift us higher up with Him. We need to press into His character and His power to step into the adventure He has for us. In the pressing in, we protect our adventure from wrongful thinking, such as:

- Another man is better for me than the husband God gave me.
- I can trim the time my children get from me and not pay a price later.
- I can cut a corner in business ethics and get away with it.
- I am above the rules.
- I can handle it when it comes to gray areas of drinking, entertainment, gambling.
- I am not vulnerable to an emotional or physical affair.
- Sex outside marriage will have no consequences if I take precautions.

Humility helps us come face-to-face with our humanity, our propensity for sin and stupidity. If we are to walk the adventure, we have to grasp our potential to destroy the adventure with our own hands. Until we grasp that we can make a mess of our world with absolutely no help from anyone else, we are not truly ready to live out the adventure.

Recently, some young women of influence and I were discussing some of the gray areas of the Christian walk. I said that we who are serious about stepping out into God's adventure for our lives must buffet our will for the sake of the adventure God has for us. I said, "The higher up we go on the ladder of leadership, the fewer choices we have." We no longer choose to do things that put ourselves, our family, or our future at risk. We protect God's adventure for our lives and the greater good of others even when it sometimes means saying "No" to our desires. The apostle Paul put it like this, "No, I beat my body and make it my slave so that after I have preached to others, I myself will not be disqualified for the prize" (1 Corinthians 9:27).

How are you doing? Make a list your shortcomings, your weaknesses, the areas of your life that have the potential to destroy your dream.

A Fortified City

In Old Testament times, cities had walls around them to protect the citizens, their homes, and their livelihoods from attack. Let's take a look at how holiness and humility can protect God's dream in our life.

Bing Hunter, author of *The God Who Hears,* describes God's moral purity as "light: blinding, unending, undiminishing, dazzling whiteness."[3] Hunter goes on to explain why holiness is so hard for us to understand:

> Christians are like fish, living in a fluid medium (society) which has become so morally murky that "light" seems abnormal. We were born in dirty water and have gotten used to it. Mud and murk are normal; clean and light are threatening. We can see rotten things on the bottom,

but assume we cannot get stuck in the muck if we keep moving. And besides, we generally swim (in circles) higher up in the pond. We have learned to live comfortably with unholiness and see lots of others wearing Ichthus pins who do too...

It is little wonder sin grieves the Holy Spirit who lives in us (Eph 4:30). Yet the greater and more astounding wonder is that sin grieves us so little.[4]

Bill Bright, founder of Campus Crusade for Christ, points out the contrast between our sin and the holiness of God:

When I think of God's holiness, I am convicted by the sinful nature of my own being. We are all like a man wearing a beautiful white suit who was invited to go down into the depths of a coal mine. In the darkness of the mine, he was not aware that his suit was becoming soiled. But when he resurfaced into the dazzling light of the noonday sun, he was fully aware that his suit had become sooty and dirty. The light of God's holiness reveals the darkness of our sin.[5]

To protect the adventure and our adventure teammates, we can't compare our behaviors and choices with that of those around us. Rather, we must weigh our decisions based upon how Christ would handle the choice.

All of life hinges on God's holiness. Without His pure, holy character, the world and all relationships would unravel.

Holiness, the Hinge on Which All of Life Hangs

Holiness is a powerful force. It is central to the character of God, and it should be central to our lives as well. Nathan Stone, in his book *The Names of God*, states that the name *Jehovah M'Kaddesh* means "dedicate, consecrate, sanctuary, hallow, and holy and...it appears [in the Bible] in its various forms some 700 times…It is of this holiness that an old Scottish divine writes: 'It is the balance…of all the attributes of Deity. Power without holiness would degenerate into cruelty; omniscience without holiness would become craft; justice without holiness would degenerate into revenge.'"[6]

All of life hinges on God's holiness. Without His pure, holy character, the world and all relationships would unravel. So what is our natural response when God reveals His perfectly just and glorious character, and we begin to wrap our mind around His holiness in comparison to our imperfection? Let's look at a few examples from people in the Bible who encountered the holiness of God.

Moses. When God revealed His glory to Moses atop Mt. Sinai, Moses was immediately inspired to obey God. Then he wanted others to experience God:

> Moses bowed to the ground at once and worshiped. "O Lord, if I have found favor in your eyes," he said, "then let the Lord go with us. Although this is a stiff-necked people, forgive our wickedness and our sin, and take us as your inheritance" (Exodus 34:8-9).

Saul. Saul too came face-to-face with the glory of God. As he neared Damascus, a light from heaven blinded him, and he fell to the ground.

> The men traveling with Saul stood there speechless; they heard the sound but did not see anyone. Saul got up from the ground, but when he opened his eyes he could see nothing. So they led him by the hand into Damascus. For three days he was blind, and did not eat or drink anything (Acts 9:7-9).

Saul's encounter with Jesus shed light on the sin in his life, and from that day forward, he would never be the same. God called him to be an apostle, and he committed his life to serve and obey God by bringing the light to the Gentiles.

Mary Magdalene. When Mary encountered Jesus outside His tomb, she did not recognize Him at first. But when she realized who He was, she fell to her knees in worship.

When we encounter God's holiness, it should affect the way we think, feel, and act.

Motivation Check

Let's push *pause* and do a motivation check on your adventure. Why are you chasing your adventure? What is your motivation? Power? Money? Fame? Prestige?

When we use our adventure to try to fill an emotional need, one that was designed for only God to fill, we become more vulnerable to the corruption of the adventure or the erosion of our team. But when we frame our dream with God's values—making the world a better place, helping others, extending God's love so people can respond to it, or the best motive of all, glorifying God—we build a fortification around the dream.

Pastor Brett Fuller prays a simple prayer each day, and I believe it holds his adventure in place and protects his marriage and family: "Lord, today help me be the best Christian I can be." If he falters on the path, the next day he simply prays, "Lord, today help me be the best Christian I can be." Then he steps out again with the resolve to walk in a manner worthy of his calling and to do all things heartily, as for the Lord.

As women on an adventure with God, we desperately need to see life through God's eyes and not our own. Bible teacher Beth Moore captures the clarifying nature of holiness when she says, "We see Him more clearly and we see ourselves more clearly."

The Choice Is Yours

When I was in college, we talked idealistically about what we proposed to do to correct the ills of society. My brother-in-law, Jim, said, "The difference between convictions and convenient beliefs are those that you will actually live out over time."

I have never forgotten that simple line. I often pray in the crux of a decision, *Lord, give me the backbone to live out the convictions You have called me to. Give me the courage to place Your call above my comfort.*

At the women's conferences I speak at, women in crisis often ask me for wisdom or advice. At one conference, two women approached me at separate times. Both were leaders I had met the year prior when I visited that area.

The first woman was in turmoil. Her church had abandoned her because her marriage was on the rocks. She told me she had been in a lifeless marriage and had gone to the church leaders for help, but none of what was offered worked. Her husband was the typical passive-aggressive, narcissistic personality (which is really painful to live with). His true colors finally revealed themselves publicly when he showed his verbally demeaning side to the leaders (this personality disorder is usually very suave and persuasive). The leaders were beginning to take her side on things, so she made the decision to move out.

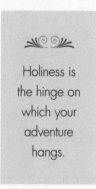

Holiness is the hinge on which your adventure hangs.

Then her husband came to the leaders and claimed she was having an affair, and church discipline was applied to *her*. She felt outraged, insulted, and maligned.

"Did you sleep with a man before your divorce was final?" I asked.

She said her marriage was dead long before and that she would have left her miserable husband anyway.

"But did you sleep with another man before your marriage officially ended?" I asked again.

"Yes," she finally confessed.

"Then you had an affair. You handed your husband the ammo he used against you. You can't blame anyone else for that part. Own your sin to be free of it."

We can blame others as much as we want, but excuses, blaming, and rationalizing will destroy our adventure, our team, and eventually our self.

At that same conference, a second woman thanked me for helping women walk away from their sin and pain and into a forward moving future. Seems she too was in a marriage with a passive-aggressive, addicted, narcissistic man, and her life with him bordered on torturous at times. She felt herself becoming emotionally attached to a sympathetic male coworker. She went on:

> I saw where my heart was taking me, and I cut all ties with that man. It was hard. I needed a friend, but what I needed more was to let God walk me through my pain and through my healing process. At one point, I told God, "I don't feel I can keep living like this, but I will choose to live my life with integrity before my children. And even though I can't trust my husband to love me, I trust You, Lord, to love me. So I will give You time to make things right for me, whatever that means."
>
> Because my husband was a narcissist and thought the world should revolve around him, when I let my life revolve around Jesus, he was angry, and he eventually had an affair and left me. It was painful, but now I'm moving forward with my life and I'm so thankful I did things God's way. My kids can look at me and know I tried everything to save the marriage. I walked with God through some pretty high waters and dark nights, but I walked with God and He walked me through. My kids know that, and my conscience is clear. I don't feel like I'm carrying as much baggage into a new relationship—if I decide to have one—and my ministry and career remained intact through all those crazy circumstances. I credit God with holding my life and my family together.

Two women with similar circumstances, yet they made two very different choices: one led to chaos, the other to clarity.

Integrity matters. Holiness is the shield that protects you when you're under attack. Holiness is the elevator that moves you up in God's economy. Holiness is the thread that will stitch you to quality people. Holiness is the hinge on which your adventure hangs.

HUMILITY

The second powerful element in making your adventure a reality is *humility*. You have been created by God with a unique combination of skills, talents, and gifts. Your life has also been a collection of experiences that have shaped your outlook and your insight into people. Humility is the acceptance of these skills and experiences as the ingredients for God's plan for your life. Micah 6:8 makes it clear that humility is a concept vital to our success:

> He has showed you, O man, what is good.
> And what does the LORD require of you?
> To act justly and to love mercy
> and to walk humbly with your God.

Rather than trying to design your own life according to your desires and imaginations, humility says, "God, I trust You with my life. I believe You made me the way You wanted me to be, and You have allowed me to experience my life so that I can have a specific influence on others. With Your help, I will seek the life You have for me." It seems that God is most pleased when we entrust our gifts and talents to Him, to His timing and for His use. As the apostle Peter exhorts us, "Humble yourselves, therefore, under God's mighty hand, that he may lift you up in due time" (1 Peter 5:6).

The word *humble* implies a posture of bowing low as in worship, stooping, or crouching. Worship is the act of acknowledging God for who He is. Humbling ourselves is a voluntary action, placing ourselves under God's hand, as a child nestles under the loving arm of a parent. From this place of shelter, the child waits and is nurtured for the challenges that lie ahead.

It is no wonder that in knowing who God is, we gain the

confidence to live our lives with the potential God has given us. "The people who know their God will display strength and take action" (Daniel 11:32 NASB). As we bow low in worship, God gives us the ability to rise and soar into our potential. We are empowered by His love.

Meek and Mighty

One of my favorite stories of a truly humble woman is the life of Harriet Beecher Stowe. She was a wife, mother, writer, and shaper of public opinion. Slavery had etched itself into Harriet's heart. She knew that it was wrong, and she had an overwhelming desire to help those who were caught in its brutality. She became active in the Underground Railroad and helped smuggle many slaves to safety and freedom. Once she even borrowed money to buy back an African-American child who had been sold to a different master than his mother. But Harriet longed to do more, something that would change hearts and save lives. But what could one woman possibly do?

One day while she was praying in church, Harriet encountered God's holiness, and suddenly her purpose was clear. In a daydream, she saw the characters and plot line of a story unroll before her. Inspired to obey the dream, Harriet, a young pastor's wife with six children, began to write the story in installments, finding time between her numerous other responsibilities. A small antislavery journal published her pieces and, more than a year after she started, Harriet completed *Uncle Tom's Cabin.* It was published in book form in 1852.

News of the compelling story traveled throughout the country— on both sides of the slavery issue. Harriet caught the attention of the nation, the president, and the world. Her novel humanized the plight of both the slave and slave owner, showing that the system abused everyone involved. The message spread like wildfire. The first day *Uncle Tom's Cabin* was released in book form, over three thousand were sold. An additional twenty thousand copies were sold in the next three weeks, and today more than three million copies of

For most of us women, the relationships we value make the adventure worth living.

the book have been distributed worldwide in 22 different languages.

People asked Harriet how a busy mom and pastor's wife could manage to also write a bestseller. She would reply, "I did not write it. God wrote it. I merely did His dictation."

You always want to be in the position to be God's conduit, His funnel, His transcriber. When you, God, and your dream team all move in the same direction, dreams come true.

YOUR HUDDLE

The third element that has the ability to energize your adventure is the vital relationships you have. Your husband (if you're married), your parents, your children, and your siblings create the adventure huddle that you negotiate adventure decisions with. Just as a quarterback returns to the huddle between plays, a wise woman will return to her adventure huddle for a sounding board for choices, prayer support, and the emotional strength to live out the adventure.

For most of us women, the relationships we value make the adventure worth living. Families of confidence make a significant difference in this world, and sometimes the ripple of influence begins with a small but powerful decision. Just ask Maria and Bob Goff. Their life-changing adventure began on a day of tragedy: 9/11. We'll let the oldest daughter, Lindsay, who is now a college student, share the story:

> Shortly after September 11, we were all sitting around the dinner table discussing current world events when Dad surprised us with a question: "Kids, if you could have five minutes in front of Pharaoh, what would you say? If you could spend time with a world leader, what would you want to ask?"

I had just learned how to make videos and loved to travel, so I said I would want to ask these leaders for a video interview and go visit them in their countries. My brother Richard said that he would want to ask these leaders about hope. In light of all of these bad things that were happening in the world, what was it that these leaders placed their hope in? Our little brother Adam said that he would want to invite these leaders over to our house. What better way to be friends than to invite someone over for a sleepover?

Dad then had us each write a letter to the current leaders of the world, which he later combined into one letter. The final product said something along the lines of, "Hi. We are Lindsey, Richard, and Adam Goff, and we are kids ages 14, 12, and 10 from San Diego, California. We would like to be friends and meet with you for a brief video interview in which you could share a message of hope and encouragement that we could share with other kids our age around the world. Could we come to your house, or would you like to come to ours?"

We downloaded the CIA website to get the names and addresses of every single world leader, and we signed, sealed, and stamped 263 letters to send out across the world.

Dad promised us that if anyone said yes, we would go. I remember talking about how many people we thought would respond. We decided that we would be really excited if one person wrote back and said "Yes." In the meantime, though, we were receiving some warm and delightful responses from different leaders saying that they loved our idea but, unfortunately, were not able to meet with us. Some wrote personal notes on the bottom of their letters and others sent photos and bookmarks. Still, we kept checking for a "yes" to come in the mail.

Then a letter arrived from the office of the vice president of Bulgaria, Angel Marin. In his letter he said, "Dear children, if you come to my office in Sofia, I would be delighted to meet with you!" A letter followed from the office of the president of Israel, Moshe Katsav, inviting us to his office in Jerusalem. Then the foreign minister of Switzerland said "yes," along with the former prime minister of Malaysia and various ambassadors and parliament members from different parts of the world. In the end, we had 29 leaders grant us interviews!

It's weird, even now, to be asked if I was fearful because the thought never entered my mind. I remember a rush of excitement and a little bit of nervousness before each interview (Would we forget all of our questions or remember the order we were supposed to ask them in?), but I was with my brothers, and we genuinely meant it when we said that we just wanted to be friends with these world leaders. Deciding to love people as friends doesn't leave any room to be fearful.

On another level, we were traveling with Dad, and he would never, never let anything bad happen to us. It's hard to see the world as a threatening place when you are being so warmly received by the people who are leading it, and when your dad is there to keep you safe.

I asked Maria, the mom, if she had any fears after making this commitment to the kids and having world leaders actually say, "Yes." She answered me candidly:

I think I was the only one in the family who felt fear and needed the most propelling. I am either the biggest chicken in the family or God has given me certain gifts of wisdom and discernment. I hope it's the latter (maybe it's both).

Yes, I was afraid to travel. If you remember back to that day on 9/11, the first defensive action our government took was to ground all commercial and private aircraft. This created the biggest no-fly zone I had ever heard of.

That made a huge impression on me. My confidence in plane transportation would never be the same.

Up until 9/11, the stories of evil terrorist attacks seemed to be a reality for other countries. The U.S. was not immune to terrorist antics, but until 9/11 it did not affect me personally. That is until we were about to take our sweet little American children on airplanes traveling to countries like Israel and Bulgaria.

It made perfect sense to me to feel fear. Fortunately, it also made perfect sense to live by faith, to fight evil with good, to go beyond our comfort zone and go out into the unknown to share God's love and light in the darkening world. I got it. We as believers need to be obedient to the work He wants us to do. It seemed more important to focus on what I could do to help fight evil than to be paralyzed by fear.

I do not normally talk about my fears as a part of the unlikely, miraculous story of how our kids reached out to world leaders. Leaders who just happened to be on watch during this time in history. It seemed to us that the world needed a soothing dose of God's love. There was no room for fear. A friend once told me that I would not find anywhere in the Bible any mention that we are to step out in faith "only if it is safe."

The Book of Philippians has been my playbook throughout most of my adult life. Philippians 4:6-7 gave me the peace and assurance I needed as our family traveled beyond our borders and comfort zone. "Do not be anxious about anything, but in everything, by prayer and petition, with thanksgiving, present your requests to God. And the peace of God, which transcends all understanding, will guard your hearts and your minds in Christ Jesus." Every request I made to God during that time was replaced with the peace that passes all understanding. If God is that faithful, I want to be too.[7]

This adventure huddle has been faithful. This family has created Restore International (www.restoreinternational.org), which is dedicated to end human rights abuses toward children worldwide.

Woman: The Heart of the Confident Home

Women with healthy relationships tend to excel, and those around them do too. Studies say children who live with a set of continuously married parents achieve better and have fewer social problems than those with divorced parents or single parents or unmarried parents.[8] It should be no surprise that women and children whose families are intact have a higher standard of living.[9] The majority of women entrepreneurs in Canada and the U.S. are married.[10]

Healthy relationships safeguard the adventure. This doesn't mean that if you are single or single again you won't reach the payoff of the adventure or that your children have to suffer. You will just need to work proactively at creating a network of successful, healthy relationships. Parents can also be a part of your adventure huddle since students with involved parents achieve better.[11] Those same supportive parents can cheer you on even in your adult world. Whether married or single, if we are surrounded by healthy, emotionally stable, supportive relationships, it will make achieving the adventure much easier.

We all need a huddle. And we need to make protecting that huddle a priority because that's what will protect the adventure God has called us to. (In the next chapter, we'll talk about the importance of your close friendships, but in this chapter, we put a priority on your adventure huddle of those primary, most vital relationships.)

Love Can Build a Dream

The people you most need to get on board with your dream are those in your adventure huddle, those relatives you are closest to. (Take a moment to list the members of your adventure huddle.)

When you, the adventurer, build into your adventure huddle, the members of your huddle become more motivated. They support you and help you in emotional and tangible ways. I hoped to gain this type of support from my husband, Bill, so I repeatedly shared with him my desire to write and make a difference among the women of my generation. I often wondered if he shared the dream because he didn't talk about it the way I did. He was calm and nonargumentative when I talked with him, but I wanted more. I wanted him to care about the dream as much as I did.

The day I knew he was on board came when we had three children and our youngest was a newborn. Bill so believed in my dream of becoming a writer that he took our last $50 and signed me up for a writers' conference. He then took care of our three children so I could attend.

To help me balance being a mom and a writer that day, Bill drove our children to me so that I could nurse my new baby midmorning, at lunch, and in the early afternoon. In between these feedings, he took them to a nearby park and kept them busy. He sacrificed so much for me that day that it became the topic of conversation at the conference.

One seasoned author said, "You want to write about relationships? Write an article about the love your husband showed today. That's the kind of love our world needs to read about and learn how to give." So I wrote it up as a newspaper article, and it has since been reprinted in numerous places. To this day it is one of the most asked for articles I have ever written.

Get Aboard the Success Train

So how can you share your adventure in such a way that your huddle can get on board, grow more cooperative, and maybe even pitch in to help achieve the adventure?

Share the Adventure. When you share the adventure and cast a vision, begin with a well-thought-out plan first. Place yourself in each family member's mind and try to answer the questions or objections you think he or she might have.

Let's look closer at my decision to reenter college after taking a break to marry and have two children. Bill and I had decided together, years before, to put him all the way through graduate school first. Then I would return and complete my undergraduate degree when I felt ready as a mom to add another responsibility to my schedule.

After we moved to a new community, I thought it might be the best time to jump back into academia. My youngest was two and my oldest was four. Ministry and friendship commitments did not yet dominate my schedule.

As I worked on my education, I also began to talk to Bill about how I would eventually apply my training. On dates we would talk about which career best matched my personality, passion, and professional work rhythm. College professor, high school teacher, freelance writer, corporate public relations, communications, and marketing were all on the whiteboard for a while. The more we talked, the more being my own boss seemed to fit my style and personal priorities.

Talk about your dream often enough that your adventure huddle is not at all surprised when you move into action.

Sensitize the Adventure. When you share the adventure, make sure you place the people you love in it. Share how your adventure, or the preparation, education, and planning for the adventure, might affect them. Share how the accomplishment of the adventure might benefit them.

When I shared the hopeful adventure to return to school with Bill, I also shared my childcare plan since he was in a brand-new pastoral role with demanding time commitments. In addition, I shared how much college would cost and how I thought we might pay for it. I had to work hard at making sure Bill and the boys didn't get lost as I fast-tracked my education. Because I had so much passion for the new adventure, I could become myopic in my conversations, and so I had to work on being more sensitive to Bill.

Structure the Adventure. Get input to tweak or adjust the adventure. After talking with Bill, I adjusted the number of units per semester to roughly equal two evenings or two mornings a week. This pace placed less stress on our marriage, family budget, and ministry. As the years rolled by, I whittled away at my units. I took a leave of absence for a year while we finished building our home and I gave birth to our third born. Then I jumped back in to finish up my senior year. Together, we decided to put my education on the fast track to get me through school and into my career, because with three children we needed a new income stream.

That semester an opportunity to write a book (coauthored with our mentors, Jim and Sally Conway) presented itself. I cut down on time spent working with a local church ministry to add in book writing time. We also decided that our sons would not play baseball that spring so we could get the book and my education completed. To thank my sons for being part of my team, at my graduation I gave them baseball caps with "Mom Did It With My Help" printed on them.

In pursuing your dream, God will ask you and those you love to adjust, so be willing to obey Him. It's part of maintaining humility and giving everyone on your team the opportunity to grasp the importance of the call on your life.

When our sons all became teens, I kept my writing and speaking schedule, but I laid down my board positions and some women's ministry responsibilities to be more available to them. Bill and I have adjusted back and forth for each other over the years. I adapted so he could finish his undergraduate and seminary degrees and establish his early career. He adapted so I could be an at-home mom, finish my college degree, and establish my writing career. I adapted so he could take several of his pastoral positions. He adapted so our team-teaching ministry could expand. It's like a tennis volley, each of us taking turns hitting so we can both succeed.

I have been fortunate that my family has, for the most part, been willing to sacrifice for me as I have been willing to sacrifice for them. But it has not always been easy. At times I have been criticized by those outside my family and resisted or teased by my adventure

> All relationships spring from the first, primary relationship with God. If something is off in that relationship, all your other relationships will suffer.

huddle for my intensity. There have been stretches of time when I had to keep working on the adventure alone with the hope that those looking in from the outside and those living it with me would see the value in the adventure walk I was taking with God.

You may find yourself in that situation often, so keep adjusting, keep seeking God's direction, and check your heart. If your heart is right before God, He will eventually bring the necessary people on board to give the adventure wings.

God is love (1 John 4:8), so relationships are very important to Him. He will guide you and your adventure huddle into His plan of love.

WINNING WORDS

To protect your huddle, humble yourself under God's mighty hand with these words in prayer:

> Follow justice and justice alone, so that you may live and possess the land the LORD your God is giving you. He will make your righteousness shine like the dawn, the justice of your cause like the noonday sun. Blessed are they who maintain justice, who constantly do what is right.
>
> When justice is done, it brings joy to the righteous but terror to evildoers. Evil men do not understand justice, but those who seek the LORD understand it fully. The righteous care about justice for the poor, but the wicked have no such concern.
>
> You must return to your God; maintain love and justice, and wait for your God always. Let justice roll on like a river, righteousness like a never-failing stream.

WINNING WISDOM

All relationships spring from the first, primary relationship with God. If something is off in that relationship, all your other relationships will suffer. God knows that because of our sin nature we have a propensity for sin and pride. Notice the *I* in the center of both words? God wants to replace self-centeredness with God-centered living because that will protect the adventure and your adventure huddle. You can experience the removal of the chains and shackles in your life by crying out to God. James 4:8 says, "Come near to God and he will come near to you." When God hears the seeker's heart, He reaches out. "For the eyes of the LORD range throughout the earth to strengthen those whose hearts are fully committed to him" (2 Chronicles 16:9). He sees your potential long before you do, and He longs to answer the heart of those who seek Him:

- But if from there you seek the LORD your God, you will find him if you look for him with all your heart and with all your soul (Deuteronomy 4:29).

- For the LORD searches every heart and understands every motive behind the thoughts. If you seek him, he will be found by you; but if you forsake him, he will reject you forever (1 Chronicles 28:9).

- I love those who love me, and those who seek me find me (Proverbs 8:17).

- The Lord is not slow in keeping his promise, as some understand slowness. He is patient with you, not wanting anyone to perish, but everyone to come to repentance (2 Peter 3:9).

WINNING WAYS

Now's a good time to do a holiness and humility check. Let's do humility first. Read this passage and then tell your fine-tuning friends or your adventure huddle in your own words what you think the verses below mean:

> [Sisters], think of what you were when you were called. Not many of you were wise by human standards; not many were influential; not many were of noble birth. But God chose the foolish things of the world to shame the wise; God chose the weak things of the world to shame the strong. He chose the lowly things of this world and the despised things—and the things that are not—to nullify the things that are, so that no one may boast before him. It is because of him that you are in Christ Jesus, who has become for us wisdom from God—that is, our righteousness, holiness and redemption. Therefore, as it is written: "Let him who boasts boast in the Lord" (1 Corinthians 1:26-31).

Who do you credit when you achieve? Go one full day or one full week and see if you can give the credit to anyone other than yourself—God, your husband, your family, your adventure team, your boss, your coworkers. See if you can deflect the credit from yourself back to God and to the people who empower you to live the dream.

Take a step of humility and holiness now and confess one personal weakness that you think could place God's adventure for your life or your adventure huddle at risk. Ask the huddle or your fine-tuning friends to pray for growth in that area.

Gather your team together and thank them for being a part of your dream. Consider doing something creative or special to acknowledge your appreciation. For my team:

> *Bill:* It takes a strong man to team with a strong woman. Your integrity is my shelter and your encouragement, my strength. I look forward to walking this dream out with you, my love. Thank you.
>
> *Brock and Hannah:* You are living proof that "those

who honor God, God honors." You are light-years ahead of your peers. Your children are blessed to have you as parents. Your employers are blessed to have you on their teams. Your integrity is a rock I can count on. Thank you.

Zach: You have worked hard to see your dream achieved, and all the while you have encouraged me in mine. Your people skills bless all those around you. Your calls of care bless me. Thank you.

Caleb: You are your father's son. In quiet strength and character you lead, and with compassion and servanthood your life has strengthened my own. Thank you.

If you could keep only those things and people you have already thanked God for today, what would be left in your life right now?[12] Pastor Jan van Olsten of New Covenant Community Church says, "There is no success without sacrifice." Stop and thank God for those in your huddle who are sacrificing for you so you can pursue God's adventurous journey.

Networking

The Synergy of Teamwork

"TEAM = Together Everyone Achieves More"

AUTHOR UNKNOWN

*Q*uality attracts quality. Be a quality person and you will attract quality people." That should have been the bumper sticker on all of our sons' cars because it was a phrase that daily rang out in our home. I truly believe we are known by the company we keep. Our influence is defined by the ground we travel and the people we travel it with. When it comes to my closest friends, they come in two sizes:

1. Those more courageous than I am and from whom I hope to catch courage.

2. Those less courageous than I am and who want to catch courage from me.

In the same way, there are two groups of people who are uncomfortable around me:

1. Women who are timid and want to keep it that way. They may be hibernating from life, huddled in the recesses of their fears or walled away from the dreams that lie dormant in their hearts.

2. The courage killers. You know them by the things they say when you share the adventure:

- What are you thinking?
- You're kidding, right?
- Oh, that can never happen.
- Oh, brother! (usually accompanied with the rolling of their eyes).
- That's a waste of time (energy, money...fill in the blank).

> I want to spend my days with those who are hungry for God and the adventures He has for their lives.

I want to be surrounded by friends who make me a better me, and I strive to be the kind of friend who encourages others to be better also. I want to be a woman who has compassion for the timid, yet gives the timid the wings and courage to soar. I want to spend my days with those who are hungry for God and the adventures He has for their lives. I want to be in the company of those who are hungry to squeeze the best out of life—women who are willing to believe that God, if He is in it, will work the adventure out and bring it to completion no matter how insurmountable it might seem. My favorite women see the vastness of the adventure and don't run from it; they run to God.

CAN YA HELP A GIRL OUT, PLEASE?

You will find that your best friends share common goals, common dreams, common values, and the common denominator of wanting the best for one another. The story of Mary and Mary is one that inspires me in my friendships.[1]

It all began when the streets were covered with ice and the radio announcer was recommending people stay off the roads. But Mary

Kay had scheduled a home demonstration of Stanley Home Products, and she had promised to show up come rain, shine, sleet, or snow. When she arrived, she soon discovered only one other person was at the party besides the hostess.

Mary Kay set aside her formal presentation and simply chatted with the two women over coffee and cake. Mary Kay noticed that the guest, Mary Crowley, had a charismatic personality. As the evening progressed, they began to compare notes on their lives.

Mary Crowley worked as the assistant to the president of a purse manufacturing company. She told Mary Kay how much she earned annually and asked her what she was making in sales. Mary Kay replied she made the same—in a very bad week. Mary Kay offered her new friend a job in sales at her company, but Mary didn't take her up on her offer.

About a month later, however, Mary called Mary Kay. Her husband was going to be stationed out of town for several months with the National Guard, and Mary wanted to try sales part-time.

Within a few months she became a full-time salesperson, and she was terrific. Because Mary was in Mary Kay's unit, the entire unit soared. And when Mary Kay was transferred to St. Louis with her husband's job, the company allowed Mary Crowley to take over Mary Kay's territory. She consistently earned huge commissions until she left to become sales manager for a new company, World Gifts.

A year later, when Mary Kay returned to Texas, she stopped to visit Mary, and this time Mary recruited Mary Kay to a position at World Gifts! Within a year, Mary Kay's unit was doing a major portion of the company's total sales.

NEW LOOK AT NETWORKING

Networking is typically seen as the making and using of relationships for one's personal gain, a kind of "I'll scratch your back if you scratch mine" mentality. The Christian, however, is challenged to a higher standard: "If you want to be great in God's kingdom, be the servant of all," and "Seek first his kingdom and his righteousness, and all these things will be given to you as well"(Matthew 6:33).

Mary Kay and Mary Crowley understood that strong networkers sincerely value people. Often God uses our love of people to create opportunity. Good networkers have an open hand with their opportunities, seeing that the best in life is a gift from God, and they are just a funnel for opportunity and good fortune. Good networkers understand that when they share opportunity, rather than selfishly hiding or holding opportunity, God multiplies the very opportunity with others.

> Good networkers have an open hand with their opportunities, seeing that the best in life is a gift from God, and they are just a funnel for opportunity and good fortune.

While at World Gifts, Mary Crowley tried to instill these ideas in her sales team of 500 women. "I taught the staff to think of the customers and hostesses as people with needs first and customers second. We had rallies, seminars, and a lot of good fellowship."

But her life was about to turn upside down. A sharp disagreement with her boss over the company's business practices led eventually to Mary's dismissal.

Mary felt unwanted and unmotivated, but it seemed God was saying, "Don't just sit there and feel sorry for yourself." Mary had taught her team to set their goals high. "Fail if you have to. Daring generates excitement, excitement generates enthusiasm, enthusiasm generates energy." Now God was holding her to it.

Mary dried her tears, put on her nicest suit, and went to see a friend who was successful in sales as well. He immediately offered her a job, but she didn't take it. What she really wanted was to start her own company, one where she could set the standards. But she wasn't sure where to start.

If I had my own company, I could set the standards I wanted upheld. I could be as generous as I wanted with commissions. What would happen if I started a business that was really dedicated to helping women create happier homes? Wouldn't it just have to succeed?

But how could I create such a company? Nobody knew me, and I didn't have the capital or contacts with suppliers. Or so I thought.

On impulse, Mary went to a large importer of decorative accessories—an importer that had supplied her previous staff with merchandise. When she walked in, she was recognized immediately and given a credit line for their products.

It seemed God was paving the path before her, but she wanted her husband's blessing. When he had left her that morning, she was in tears on the sofa. That evening he found her bubbling over with excitement. "Honey, if you don't go into business," he told her, "the world of business will be the loser."

> "When you put God first, family second, and your career third, everything seems to work out."

Mary's company, Home Interiors and Gifts, was a huge success. Mary found herself invited to the White House, giving away Christmas shopping sprees, supporting many charitable causes, funding the start-up of a company owned and operated by the disabled, and funding an entire new building for children at her church.

PEOPLE ARE THE PRODUCT

Like Mary Crowley, Mary Kay wanted to create opportunities for others. After spending 25 years as a professional saleswoman, Mary Kay retired and decided to create her own company that offered women a chance to achieve their dreams and goals. "My objective was to give women the opportunity to do anything they were smart enough to do. And so to me, 'P and L' meant more than profit and loss; it meant people and love."

Mary Kay founded Mary Kay Cosmetics on her down-home Southern values rooted in biblical truths. "When you put God first, family second, and your career third, everything seems to work out." Mary Kay wanted to be at the helm of a company that was run by the golden rule ("Do to others as you would have them do to you"—Luke 6:31), and so she is adamant about encouraging her employees to support and praise each other. Being positive and enthusiastic is a company mantra.

> "Often it's the little, daily decisions—the ones you make hour by hour—that mean the difference between success and failure."

"It's a really good day to me if just one more woman discovers how great she really is and how much potential she has," Mary Kay says.

> One of the most important steps I ever took was when I began imagining that every single person I met had a sign around his or her neck that read, "Make me feel important." Whether it's figuratively or literal—absolutely everyone responds to applause. I believe that if you had the choice of two gifts for your child—$1 million on one side of the scale and the ability to think positively on the other—the greater gift would be the gift of confidence. And you only give confidence with praise and applause.

Mary Kay's principles and values paid off. In 1984 Mary Kay Cosmetics was named one of the 100 best companies to work for in America.

NETWORK WITH GOD FIRST

The source of Mary Kay's and Mary Crowley's enthusiasm and positive attitudes can be traced back to their most important relationship—their relationship with God. "I believe we have found success because God has led us all the way," Mary Kay says. "Often it's the little, daily decisions—the ones you make hour by hour—that mean the difference between success and failure. And I feel that God put His protective arm around us and guided us to the right path."

Both Marys have been honored with the Horatio Alger Award, an award that recognizes Americans who are committed to sharing a message of hope and encouragement. In receiving their awards, they both reinforced the importance of knowing God and seeing people as God sees them. In her acceptance speech, Mary Crowley enthusiastically said, "I think one person with belief is equal to a force of 99 with only an interest. And I have belief. I believe in the Creator who made me in His image. Because of that fact, I am 'somebody.' Consequently, I am able to look at everybody else as a 'somebody' too."

Mary Kay was asked by *60 Minutes* host Morley Safer, "Now, I have been around here a couple of days, and every time I turn around I hear the word *God*. Aren't you really just using God?" Mary Kay looked him squarely in the eye and gently replied, "No, Mr. Safer, I sincerely hope it's the other way around—that God is using me."

In networking, God brings people together and uses their lives to spread the opportunity to experience His love and joy. He took Mary Kay's ordinary faithful commitment as a salesperson for Stanley Home Products and turned it into an extraordinary connection. Mary and Mary were both better and more successful because they knew one another. True networking is a win-win for all involved.

HOLD ME ACCOUNTABLE!

A woman of confidence needs to have an accountability partner—someone she can trust to be honest with her about her strengths and her weaknesses, someone who will encourage her in the hard times and rejoice in the good. I like to think of an accountability partner as a fine-tuning friend, like the electronic tuner my husband uses to tune his guitar. He can judge pretty well by ear if the guitar is in tune, but the tuner makes it even more precise. The same is true of a woman who has a few good fine-tuning friends.

Accountability is not a word you will find in the Bible, but the principle of accountability is found in the term *exhortation*, which means "called alongside to bring out the best in another." It carries the idea of compassionate encouragement. *Admonish* is another biblical term that describes the principle of accountability. It literally means "to put in mind" and carries the idea of putting the right thoughts into the minds of others.

A few well-chosen, fine-tuning friends can become a great source of strength for you, but it works only if you want it to. The condition of your heart is vital to the success of an accountability relationship. A tender, contrite, repentant heart that wants God's best and God's growth is fertile ground. Your ready heart is the instrument God needs in order to use your fine-tuning friend to tune you to His will. In the preface I encouraged you to gather your girlfriends together to do this study because I believe that together we women are stronger. These women, along with your family (your *adventure huddle*), will become your *adventure team*.

If you've ever rock climbed or rappelled, you probably strapped on a harness and connected yourself with ropes and carabiners to others. This is to keep you safe, to keep you from plummeting to your death. In the same way, your adventure team is a safeguard to your adventure and to your family, your life, and your future. Use them. Gain from their wisdom, experience, advice, and prayers.

If you haven't gathered this team of girlfriends yet, make a few calls, send a few e-mails, and get together for a prayer walk or coffee and lay out your need for them in your life. Some will say yes; others will not be able to handle the time commitment. But God knows who you need in your corner for you to succeed. It is His responsibility to gather the team; it is your responsibility to ask these sisters to join you on the journey. The best adventure teams are made up of women who all want to be on God's adventure, and so they hold each other accountable, and they all grow, blossom, and succeed. Everyone gains.

> I need to be surrounded by positive women but not "yes women." That's not a safety net to my adventure; honesty is.

FINDING A FINE-TUNING FRIEND

When you look for a fine-tuning friend, here are a few questions to consider:

- Is she a friend you'd like to spend more time with?
- Is she enough a part of your world to see your marriage and your interactions with children, coworkers, and volunteers?
- Can this woman keep confidences?
- Does she have credibility in your eyes?
- Has she been through the fire? Do you respect her?
- Does she know Jesus as well or better than you do?
- Will she be a prayer advocate who will consistently lift you and your concerns to your Father in heaven?

I have found these traits most helpful for honing me. For example, I need a friend who knows Christ at about my level so that, as I struggle through life issues, I know she will send me to Scriptures that will get my attention. I need her to be a woman who has gone through trials in her life so that she can relate to me when I hit my own. As I see how a woman goes through tough times, I gain respect and confidence that she will have something to say when I hit my own bumps in the road.

I also need women in my world who carry similar responsibilities as I do. Those who don't carry a similar load hear about my life and feel overwhelmed and may be too intimidated to offer advice.

I need to be surrounded by positive women but not "yes women" who agree with an idea simply because I said it. That's not a safety net to my adventure; honesty is.

However, the two imperative traits are her abilities to keep a confidence and to pray for me consistently. Prayer is how any forward movement in life is won, and I need a friend I can honestly share specifics with so we can commit them to prayer and trust God to give His answers in His way at His time.

One of the most important first prayers of a woman of confidence who desires to achieve with integrity is, "Lord, send me a fine-tuning friend!"

QUESTIONS TO HELP YOU FINE-TUNE EACH OTHER

At one retreat I attended, the women were encouraged to find someone who could become an accountability partner. They were given a bookmark with this list of questions to carry in their Bibles, and I suggest you use these questions when you talk with your fine-tuning friend about your lives.

1. Have you talked to someone about Jesus this week?

2. Have you managed your time wisely?

3. Have you taken time to thank the Lord this week? Have you had your quiet times?

4. Have you had a good attitude toward your spouse and children this week?

5. Have you said damaging things about another person, either behind their back or to their face?

6. Have you succumbed to a personal addiction?

7. Have you continued to remain angry toward another?

8. Have you fantasized a romantic relationship with

someone other than your spouse or read or seen any
sexually alluring material?

9. Have you lacked integrity in your financial dealings?
Have you spent recklessly?

10. Have you secretly wished for another's misfortune so
that you might excel?

11. Have you been completely truthful with me just now?

The next year at the same retreat, I got to hear the results from
the women who found an accountability partner or fine-tuning
friend and who asked these questions on a regular basis. Many came
to personal faith, affairs were ended, parenting skills and confidence
in mothering increased, businesses started running according to
God's principles, addictive behaviors ceased, new companies and
ministries were launched, marriages were saved, and so on. Excitement permeated the room as women shared, and I believe they
were excited because they had a clear conscience, knowing they had
achieved with integrity.

WHEN YOU ARE THE TUNER

Confronting in love is never easy, but I use this simple exercise to
better prepare me when I feel God asking me to confront a friend.

Know. Write down the facts, what you know about an issue. For
example, you might write, "I know you slammed the door, yelled,
and then threw down your briefcase." Do not try to guess why. Just
write down the facts, not any interpretation of actions or reactions.

The most important observation is that of my own feelings,
motives, and stresses about the friend or issue. I ask myself, "Is this
even my issue? Have I earned the right to speak into her life? Am
I the best person to do this? Am I doing this because of an unmet
emotional need in my own life?" My rule is, "If in doubt, don't
confront." However, if I sense my concern and care is exactly what
God wants, I pray through my own fears till I reach obedience. I
wait for God's green light.

Feel. How do you feel about this issue? How do you think she is feeling? I try to walk a mile in her pumps. By looking at life through her eyes, I usually get a sense of whether I need to encourage, confront, or remain silent and pray. God usually gives me a sense of timing about what I should or shouldn't say and when I should or shouldn't say it.

> My fine-tuning friends have held me up in prayer, through honest words, and with actions.

Do. What are some options? Brainstorm and make a "problems to solve" list. I also create a "questions to ask" list. I don't want to begin by accusing. Rather, I seek to gain information for greater understanding. I try to come up with as many positive options as I can to see if there might be a win-win solution or a way to present the issue and allow my friend to come to her own godly conclusions.

When it comes time to meet with my friend, I review what Jesus said to His disciples about confronting a believer:

> "If your brother sins against you, go and show him his fault, just between the two of you. If he listens to you, you have won your brother over. But if he will not listen, take one or two others along, so that 'every matter may be established by the testimony of two or three witnesses.' If he refuses to listen to them, tell it to the church; and if he refuses to listen even to the church, treat him as you would a pagan or a tax collector" (Matthew 18:15-17).

Then I follow the steps He laid out in this passage:

1. Go privately. If your message is received well, you've won a friend.

2. If the first meeting didn't go well, go with another person who is credible and close to the friend.

3. If step two doesn't bring your friend back to God, bring the issue to a small group of believers who will walk alongside the friend if she does repent and return to Christ. Choose these friends with the same standards you would use to choose a fine-tuning friend.

4. If the friend still does not repent, treat her as someone who does not know Jesus and show her His love.

WHEN YOU ARE BEING TUNED UP

Sometimes being tuned up is even harder than tuning others. When you are confronted by one of your fine-tuning friends, try to follow these guidelines for receiving her message:

1. Receive it with grace no matter how it is given.

2. Don't take it personally no matter how personal the critique.

3. Consider the source. My fine-tuning friend receives a greater hearing in my heart than an unsigned letter or a person with gaping blind spots in her own life.

4. Consider the number of messengers. Counselor E. Dixon Murrah puts it this way: "If someone says you have a tail, think about it. If two people tell you you have a tail, think about it more seriously. But if three people tell you you have a tail, go look in the mirror."[2]

5. Talk to your Father in heaven about it.

6. If it's a lie, take it captive and refuse to receive it emotionally.

7. If it's from God, He has usually brought it up already in other times or places and through His Word. Ask Him to let you know how to proceed with this new information and to heal any emotional hurts.

As a woman who desires achievement, as a woman who wants to walk God's adventure for her life, you need trusted friends who can hold you up. My fine-tuning friends have held me up in prayer, through honest words, and with actions.

Recently my best friend, the one who can read the stress on my face and even hear it in my voice over the phone, sent me a copy of the same e-mail I had sent to her three years before after my father died. It was an e-mail that listed four areas of life I needed (and still need) her to hold me accountable for. But it was also a thank you. Here are a few of the opening lines:

> Thanks for being such a good friend. I have been reflecting lately, and I think that you are the closest thing to a best friend I have ever had. I just don't let myself be totally open and real with many people. But I am learning to be with you because you ask me. You pick up on things. You are so clued in to my pain because we had some kindred experiences growing up and similar things trigger us. Anyway, I wanted to thank you for something very small and natural on your part that meant much to me…Even though you didn't know it, I needed that expression of friendship (I didn't even know it until it was given). Thanks for being willing to be patient as I learn to be more candid.

My friend and I have encouraged one another through all kinds of seasons in our lives, including issues with our children, the deaths of family members, health issues, and personal issues. We have celebrated my first book and celebrated again many years later when another hit the bestseller list. We have rejoiced over our children's and husbands' triumphs. We have rejoiced even more over personal triumphs won by prayer in battles that almost no one else even knew about. Because we have committed ourselves to being women who make a difference in this world, we are kindred spirits intent on keeping our integrity. Our relationship of honesty keeps us moving forward in confidence.

She has prayed me through many a book and many a speaking engagement. She is now praying for me as I tackle the "battle of the bulge." I have encouraged her as she has faced down her fears and stepped into the confidence God had waiting for her.

SISTERING

Years ago when we built our home, we hammered two-by-fours together on bearing walls and around doors and windows so they could hold more weight. We later discovered that the building term for this is *sistering*. Isn't that what women of all ages and stages of life need, sisters who can come alongside and help bear our burdens and cheer us on as we walk out God's adventure for our lives? Get yourself some "sisters," some fine-tuning friends, and the adventure will seem more possible—and a whole lot more fun! After all, you need sisters to celebrate with you when you succeed in life's adventure, right?[3]

> We need sisters who can come alongside and help bear our burdens and cheer us on as we walk out God's adventure for our lives.

WINNING WORDS

Turn, O LORD, and deliver me; save me because of your unfailing love. Show the wonder of your great love, you who save by your right hand those who take refuge in you from their foes. I love you, O LORD, my strength. For the king trusts in the LORD; through the unfailing love of the Most High he will not be shaken. For your love is ever before me, and I walk continually in your truth. Let your face shine on your servant; save me in your unfailing love. Many are the woes of the wicked, but the LORD's unfailing love surrounds the man who trusts in him. But the eyes of the LORD are on those who fear him, on those whose hope is in his unfailing love.

May your unfailing love rest upon us, O LORD, even as we put our hope in you. Continue your love to those who know you, your righteousness to the upright in heart. Rise up and help us; redeem us because of your unfailing love. For great is your love, reaching to the heavens; your faithfulness reaches to the skies. But I will sing of your strength, in the morning I will sing of your love; for you are my fortress, my refuge in times of trouble. When I said, "My foot is slipping," your love, O LORD, supported me. May your unfailing love be my comfort, according to your promise to your servant. Let the morning bring me word of your unfailing love, for I have put my trust in you. Show me the way I should go, for to you I lift up my soul. The LORD delights in those who fear him, who put their hope in his unfailing love.

𝒲INNING WISDOM

My friend Linda said to me once, "I don't network; I make friends." I use this to check my motive on how I treat people who could have a positive impact on my life if they were a part of my world. I like to view networking as an opportunity to serve others. It is my goal to help others succeed, and I trust that God will bless that servant's attitude and give me what I need when I need it.

Bestselling author Carol Kent echoed this sentiment in an address to leaders. She included this statement in her list of things she wished she had known early in her career: "I wish I had realized earlier that when you open doors for others, God always opens doors for you." This isn't the reason we network but rather the natural result of networking. When we have a servant's heart, we place ourselves under God's umbrella of blessing.

Much is accomplished with a teamwork attitude. Here are some quotes on teamwork to ponder:[4]

- "There is no *I* in *teamwork*."—Unknown
- "Teamwork: Simply stated, it is less me and more we."—Unknown
- "None of us is as smart as all of us."—Ken Blanchard

- "Coming together is a beginning; keeping together is progress; working together is success."—Henry Ford
- "A group becomes a team when each member is sure enough of himself and his contribution to praise the skills of the others."—Norman Shidle
- "There is no such thing as a self-made man. You will reach your goals only with the help of others."—George Shinn

Which statement expresses an area you'd like to improve?

God has called me to make connections to Himself, to opportunities, and to others. How about you? How do you handle your friendships? The book of Proverbs says, "Iron sharpens iron, so one man sharpens another" (27:17). Use the questions below to do a friendship check on how you treat others:

- Do I seek to bring out the best in others, even if it means they will outshine me?
- Do I do unto others as I would have done unto me?
- Do I keep confidences?
- Do I promote unity and win-win outcomes?
- Do I try to reciprocate when loyalty, favors, and appreciation are given to me?
- Do I desire to create opportunities rather than obstacles for others?

𝒲INNING WAYS

With your adventure team, discuss the Winning Wisdom questions, then take teamwork to the next level. Ask each other how much of a servant you are being on your adventure. Here are a few verses to consider as you discuss servant-based success:

- "A student is not above his teacher, nor a servant above his master" (Matthew 10:24).
- "The greatest among you will be your servant" (Matthew 23:11).
- "His master replied, 'Well done, good and faithful servant! You have been faithful with a few things; I will put you in charge of many things. Come and share your master's happiness!'" (Matthew 25:21).
- "No servant can serve two masters. Either he will hate the one and love the other, or he will be devoted to the one and despise the other. You cannot serve both God and Money" (Luke 16:13).
- "If anyone wants to be first, he must be the very last, and the servant of all" (Mark 9:35).

Once you have a handle on the attitude of being a servant, it's time to write a personal mission statement. Sometimes writing a personal motto or a creed of purpose helps keep us on track when it comes to serving others. My personal mission is to encourage and equip women to be all God designed them to be. Mary Crowley had many short statements that served as guideposts to her life and business. Mary chose some life essentials:

- Learning to develop your character in God's image
- Faithfulness in your family life
- Absolute honesty on the job
- Helping those who need you[5]

My personal motto is also the same motto that Bill and I used to raise our children: "Those who honor God, God honors" (a paraphrase of 1 Samuel 2:30). One Christmas when the kids were in college, I knew they didn't have funds for gifts, so I told the guys, "All I want for Christmas are words that will make me cry." As a surprise to me, Bill worked with the guys, asking them to send him their letters. Bill then superimposed each letter over a picture of that son playing his favorite sport. It was interesting on Christmas morning when each read their "tribute" to me. All three of them, unprompted by Bill and unbeknownst to the others, had included the line, "Thanks for teaching me that 'Those who honor God, God honors.'"

Your motto should be contagious and help others make wiser choices in relationships and integrity. One of the young women I mentor heard her mother say to her every morning as she left for school,

> May the words of my mouth and the meditation
> of my heart
> Be pleasing in your sight,
> O LORD, my Rock and my Redeemer.
>
> (Psalm 19:14)

Years later that line plays in the back of her mind and helps her make clear relational decisions.

Have you written a personal motto or defined the principles that will guide your actions? With your fine-tuning friends (and your adventure team), discuss what principles guide your life. By writing a mission statement and boiling it down to a personal motto of one sentence (or two), you gain a compass for the adventure.

Take the time to write a mission statement that captures your heart and passion. Enlist the help of your adventure team to write your mission and motto if you'd like. After it's in final form, share it with your team. Then frame it, engrave it onto something for your desk or office, or place it on your business card holder and carry it with you in a briefcase or purse.

Choose an appropriate Bible verse as an integrity reminder and read it when you're tempted to treat people less kindly. Commit this verse to memory or write it out and place it next to your mission statement so that you will have a daily reminder of who you are before God.

Our son Brock won numerous awards in high school and college, so we asked him what motivated him to achieve that level of excellence. "You encouraged me to have a dream big enough to make wise choices for," he said.

Sisters, make your adventure big enough to make wise choices for. These tools—fine-tuning friends, a mission statement, a motto, and wisdom from the Bible—will remind you of the big adventure God has for you and how to stay on the trail as you walk it out to fulfillment.

Everyone on the way to the pinnacle needs a good compass.

STEP into God's Adventure

Speak the Adventure
Team up for the Adventure
Energize the Adventure
Push the Adventure

Energize the Adventure

It's a Mind Game

"A woman is like a teabag: Only in hot
water do you realize how strong she is."

NANCY REAGAN

r. J.P. Moreland says, "Make no mistake, like it or not, we are in a war for the hearts, minds and destinies of men and women all around us."[1] All of us who are holding an adventure in our hearts will pursue that adventure amidst a battle. The tendency when you are under duress is to rely on your own abilities to navigate through the storm. There are, however, three tools that will make supernatural abilities available to you at just the right time in your dream building. These three tools are God's peace, God's perspective, and God's power.

GOD'S PEACE

The first tool that will keep the adventure alive in the battlefield of life is *God's peace*. To live with peace of mind, you must make up your mind that God is able *before* the crisis or stress hits. One day in my life is a pivotal picture of this truth:

I had been out running errands. As I walked into the house, the phone was ringing. It was the phone call that no mother ever wants to receive.

"Pam!" said my husband, Bill. He sounded scared, and he struggled with the words he was weighing out. "The sheriff wants you to bring as many photos of Caleb as you can find. Pam, the boys are missing."

I hung up the phone and burst into tears. My Caleb was only five years old. How could he be missing? He had been at his best friend's house playing, and now he and his friend were gone.

Unexpected Peace

I looked around for photos of Caleb, but I couldn't see any. My eyes blurred with tears of panic. *God, Caleb needs me right now. I need to find pictures. Please be with my Caleb, and help me be the kind of mom Caleb needs. Give me Your peace.*

We tend to see peace as the absence of trouble; rather, peace is God's calming presence in the midst of trouble.

A supernatural calm entered my soul, and as I looked up, I could see photos of Caleb all over the wall and on the shelf. I grabbed them and ran out the door.

As I headed across town, I panicked again. *What was he wearing? What did I put on him this morning?* I couldn't remember. *I must be a terrible mother. I can't even remember what I put on my little boy! God, I need Your peace! I can't think. God, please help me be the kind of mom Caleb needs. Help me remember. Give me peace so I can think. Protect Caleb and give him peace.*

Then I remembered: Caleb was wearing a striped shirt, black sweatpants, brown boots—and that wonderful curly blond hair. Tears flowed down my cheeks, and I blinked and frantically wiped my eyes so I could see the road. *God, give me Your peace. Help me make it to Gail's safely.*

I thought of my friend Gail, and I empathized with how frantic she must be feeling as well. What would I say to her? I knew she was an attentive and caring mom. *She's probably as freaked out as I am right now,* I thought. *God, what am I going to say to her? Give Gail peace. Help me be the kind of friend I need to be right now. Be with our two little boys. Give them Your peace and protection.*

As I turned the corner, I saw Gail in the center of her yard. I ran from my car, wrapped my arms around her, and said, "Gail, I love you. We will get through this together." We begged God to watch over the boys and to give us peace so we could be strong. Patrol cars were speeding to the scene as my husband appeared from behind the house.

"Not there, either," he said.

Then he saw me. He wrapped his arms around me, and he prayed, "God, help us find our precious Caleb."

The sheriff interrupted. "We're sending out all available squad cars, and they have dispatched two helicopters. Are those the pictures of your children?" He asked a few more questions, then said, "We would like one parent of each child to stay here with me at the command post." Bill suggested that Gail and I stay while he volunteered to lead the charge into the countryside of overgrown brush filled with transients, wild animals, and even criminals.

I called my friend Penny and had her call Neighborhood Watch, the school, the people in our church, and her mom's friends in the adjoining retirement community. My two older sons, Brock and Zach, went together through the neighborhood and caught kids coming off school buses to tell them to keep an eye out. Worried parents appeared from their homes to help in the search. Soon hundreds of volunteers were out looking for two lost five-year-old boys.

When Brock and Zach returned, I sent them home with one of my best friends in case Caleb had tried walking home, five miles away. As they pulled away, I saw their worried faces peering back at me. The panic and fear began to rise again. *Lord, please give Brock and Zach peace. I can't see them or Bill, and they can't see me. And Caleb can't see any of us! We all need your peace!*

The sheriff in command asked me, "What time is it, Mrs.

Farrel?" I looked at my watch—two hours had already passed. Soon two helicopters appeared overhead, announcing a description of our missing boys. I looked at Gail. Tears were streaming down both our faces. This was real. This was a nightmare.

God, be with Caleb. I know Your Word. You say all things are held in the palm of Your hand. You say that all the angels are at Your command. Send Your angels. Protect those boys. Be with my Caleb. He knows You, and Your Spirit resides inside him. Give him Your peace. Wrap Your love around him. And God be with Bill too. Give him Your peace. God, help me be the kind of mom I need to be. Give me Your peace, Your strength, Your hope.

A supernatural calm reassured my heart once again.

"Mrs. Farrel, what time is it?" the officer asked. I told him again. Over three hours had gone by. I began to cry as I sensed precious time ebbing away. I prayed, *God, You know all things. I take my stand in You and Your shed blood on the cross. I command that all evil be sent away through Your power.* The peace returned, and I continued to pray for Caleb and direct the stream of new volunteers that kept arriving.

"Mrs. Farrel, what time is it?" the officer asked again. I wanted to scream at him, "Get a watch!" But I didn't. I looked at my watch, told the officer the time, and continued to pray.

"It's been four hours," the officer said. "If we don't find the boys in the next few minutes, we'll have to go down the street to the fire station and set up a permanent command post."

The words slapped me in the face. This was bad news. This was the loss of hope. This was the beginning of the end.

God, You say You are in control, and I believe that. I'm going to choose right now that no matter what happens, I will hang on to You. I know the only hope and help for my family is to believe You are who You say You are. God, Your Word says that You are good. It says You can turn dark into light and work all things together for good, so right now I choose to believe. And even if they bring my precious Caleb to me dead, I will choose to believe the truth of who You are. I can choose despair or I can choose

You. I choose You. Give us Your presence—Caleb, Bill, Brock, Zach, and me. God, I am claiming and standing in Your peace.

I saw a squad car pull up and two officers talking. The commander approached.

"We have received a sighting of two youths. We don't have any confirmation, but we are sending a squad car to see if the two children are your sons. Please, we don't have confirmation."

"But we have hope," I said, smiling.

The time ticked by. Gail and I continued to pray for God's peace. Bill heard the news and came running back to the house. About twenty minutes later, a squad car pulled up. Two doors popped open and out tumbled two tousled, dirty boys—our boys! I ran to Caleb. I wrapped my arms around him and said, "I love you, Caleb!"

I heard a quiet but relieved "I love you, Mommy."

Bill gave him a hug and they exchanged "I love you's," and then we asked, "Where have you been?"

Here's a recap of what Caleb told us.

He and his friend were eating fresh-baked cookies on the front patio when Gail stepped inside to check on her last batch. "You want to go on a great adventure?" Gail's five-year-old son asked Caleb. Caleb quickly agreed, and off they went around the corner and down the street a few blocks.

The boys stopped to play on some playground equipment at an apartment complex nearby. Then Caleb's friend saw a mobile-home park across the street and said, "My babysitter lives there. Let's go see her!" (She actually lived in a mobile-home park in another city.) The boys sped across the street, played in some people's yards, and then went into a huge culvert where they stayed for the hours we were looking for them. The boys finally popped their heads out of the storm tunnel, and the manager of the mobile-home park spotted them.

God's peace brings sanity in insane situations.

That was the longest day of my life—but God gave peace. The same peace that I've seen Him give to parents at hospital bedsides, and the same peace He gives at the graveside. Supernatural peace that goes beyond comprehension. God's peace brings sanity in insane situations. God's peace is solid when it feels as if you've just stepped into quicksand. I didn't know that day what the outcome would be, but I knew my only hope for that moment, or the moments ahead, was in banking on the character of God, the giver of peace.

Walk Out Peace

British theologian Charles Price shares a story of a painting contest in England in which the theme was peace. Most of the paintings depicted serene settings. The winning painting, however, depicted a raging storm beating against a cliff. Tucked into the cleft of a rock on the cliff was one tiny nest. A ray of light broke through the dark storm clouds and illumined the nest where a gull was peacefully sleeping, safe from the torrential surroundings.

We tend to see peace as the absence of trouble; rather, peace is God's calming presence in the midst of trouble. The Bible tells us that one of God's names is Jehovah Shalom, meaning "the Lord is our peace." Time and again the Bible acknowledges God as the giver of peace. I am so grateful that I had Jesus the day Caleb was missing. My relationship with God pulled me through. His very presence brought us peace.

Peace can be hard to come by along the adventure trail. Before you begin an adventure, you might lose sleep pondering, planning, or worrying about the possibilities. Once you begin walking the adventure, you may have to deal with people issues, financial concerns, or unforeseen obstacles. These too can rob your peace. No matter the cause, the solution is the same: Tuck yourself under God's protective wing by focusing on His ability to bring peace, no matter what the problem is. We do this by parking ourselves right in the middle of the character of God.

In John 15 we are encouraged to remain or abide in Christ. The word *abide* means "to dwell or pitch a tent." The goal is to drive in the stakes of your mind and "camp out" on God, His strength, His power, His attributes, and His character. The moment my eyes open in the morning, my mind often begins to reel through the concerns of the coming day, and the responsibilities crush down on me. So I have made it a habit to recount the attributes and character of God before my feet even hit the floor. Before I get out of bed, I've already camped out in the person of God.

In John 15:11 the result of abiding is unwrapped: "I have told you this so that my joy may be in you and that your joy may be complete." When you camp out in who God is, you get joy. The power of abiding in Christ is echoed in Isaiah 26:3 (ESV):

> You keep him in perfect peace
> whose mind is stayed on you,
> because he trusts in you.

The word *stay* means "to lean, lay, rest...lean upon."[2] When times are tough, I will post the names or the traits of God on cards or Post-it notes so I am consistently reminded that God is still in control even if life feels out of control.

Paul tells us in Philippians 4:6-7, "Do not be anxious about anything, but in everything, by prayer and petition, with thanksgiving, present your requests to God. And the peace of God, which transcends all understanding, will guard your hearts and your minds in Christ Jesus." So when we camp out in God by focusing on who He is, praising Him, and praying fervently, the peace that guards is the result.

True strength comes not from having life under our control but from the surety that life is under God's control.

I have learned that true strength comes not from having life under our control but from the surety that life is under God's control. Then and only then can we find inner peace.

Praying the Peace

When you are struggling to hold on to your inner peace, it helps to pray verses out loud, proclaiming Christ's peace over your life:

> The LORD turn his face toward you and give you peace. May there be the LORD's peace forever. The LORD gives strength to his people; the LORD blesses his people with peace. Peace I leave with you; my peace I give you...Do not let your hearts be troubled and do not be afraid. I have told you these things, so that in me you may have peace. We have peace with God through our Lord Jesus Christ...and we rejoice in the hope of the glory of God. For God is not a God of disorder but of peace. For he himself is our peace. And the peace of God, which transcends all understanding, will guard your hearts and your minds in Christ Jesus. Let the peace of Christ rule in your hearts, since as members of one body you were called to peace. Now may the Lord of peace himself give you peace at all times and in every way.

GOD'S PERSPECTIVE

The second tool that will keep your adventure alive when the heat is on is *God's perspective* on life. In a conversation with Jill Briscoe about the attacks that come to each of us, she said, "If Satan can't destroy the dream, he will try to destroy the dreamer."

"And if he can't get to the dreamer," I said, "he'll try for the dreamer's spouse; and if he can't get to the spouse, he'll try for the kids; and if he can't get the kids, he'll try for her staff; and if he can't get the staff, he'll try for the staff's family; and if he can't get the staff's family, he'll try for the dreamer's car, refrigerator, computer, or washing machine!"

Walk with Perspective

When an attack hits, the healthiest thing to do is to try to gain Christ's perspective on the attack. Sometimes that requires a gradual process of moving from your pain into God's provision, as Monique's story illustrates so well.

When I first met Monique, I noticed that she was bright and articulate. I soon learned that she was the co-owner of a business worth about a million dollars. She seemed like a woman who had it all, but I saw a pain in her eyes and a wounded spirit that she tried to cover with bravado.

Monique expressed an interest in spiritual things and soon began to attend church. Because she wanted the best out of life, she quickly realized that knowing God was the best choice for her and her family, and so she recommitted her life to Christ. As Monique grew in her faith, she began to wonder if her priorities were in line with God's.

> I controlled much of the day-to-day operations, administration, and financial responsibilities of the company. The pressure to perform and stay on top was incredible. I asked my husband, "When is enough enough?" He had no answer.
>
> I was finally getting the inkling that while I was working toward an end—a comfortable living with the opportunity to live in a bigger house, maybe have a few vacations a year, and decide when we were going to retire—my husband's work *was* his end. There was no other aspiration for him. It just had to be bigger and bigger, more and more. He had become just like his workaholic father.
>
> I had been a willing partner in this elusive race for accumulating more and more. I knew at some point, it had to stop.
>
> God shuffled the deck of my priorities so my kids and spiritual life began to take my time and energy. I was finding strength in God, and I was also finding a new freedom from the tyranny of having to always do bigger and better for the company. God was now in control of me rather than the company.[3]

A Change of View

Monique also began to notice an unhealthy pattern at work and at home:

> While running the company I was always the one who disciplined, counseled, directed the staff. He was the good guy that everyone could talk to. He would come into my office, shut the door, then go into a rage about something, wanting me to confront and deal with whatever issue it was. I would open the door and handle whatever it was. He maintained his good guy image while I played the bad guy. At the time I thought it was for the good of the company and simply the way things worked. As I became more in touch with the Lord, I became uncomfortable with the "bad boss" role. I tried to talk to my husband about it, and he would have nothing to do with changing it.

Monique was realizing more and more each day that her life was out of perspective. Her marriage had some serious flaws as well. She was being held captive by her husband's compulsive need for sexual gratification and his addictive behaviors.

> When he didn't get the sex he wanted, he would go to work in a terrible mood, causing havoc within the company. Only he and I knew why. It felt like emotional blackmail. It felt like pay up or lose all we've worked for. Give in whenever and wherever. I felt like I was between a rock and a hard place, but I was committed to our marriage, our family, and my husband. I wanted the best for us.

At about the time Monique was questioning things in her life, an old friend reentered the picture:

> Sharon had first come into our lives as a childcare provider I found through a referral service. We eventually talked to her about coming to work in sales for us, which she did.

Shortly thereafter she started having trouble in her marriage. Her husband had slept with her best friend, and she came to me for help and guidance. Over the next year we were very supportive, taking much time from very busy days to help dry her tears and prop her up emotionally and financially. The business flourished through this time with the three of us working so hard.

Monique was hoping that all the hard work would pay off and that her marriage would also flourish. At a marriage conference, she decided that God wanted her to help her husband by not giving in to his sexual addiction and irrational control:

I made a decision to no longer let his mood affect my moods. I knew I wasn't the one who could fill the void in his heart and life. That was something only God could do. I felt I needed to keep the world my kids and I dwelt in more healthy, not tossed around or controlled by one person's negativity and unhealthy behaviors.

Sharon was a close friend by then, and she helped me to make this paradigm shift. As I think back on it now, I should have known better than to seek her counsel. There were so many things in her life not to respect. She dressed provocatively, rarely kept good friends for long periods of time, and she did not have a personal relationship with God.

Monique calmly explained her decision to her husband, and he seemed almost too eager to agree to the change in their relationship. Company business led him out of town more and more, and when he went, Sharon would also go. More and more of their family time became entwined with Sharon and her children. Around Christmas, Monique began to notice even more bizarre behaviors. Her husband didn't want to sleep in their bed, avoided spending time with her and the children, and began to have fits of rage that escalated in intensity.

Monique became alarmed. She asked her husband to go for counseling and to speak to their pastor, but he refused. Even when their pastor stopped by their home or made other attempts to talk to him, her husband refused to communicate. She asked him to tell her what was going on in his mind, but he still refused. Instead, one day she was served divorce papers. The deception was unmasked.

> I found out that the woman who had cared for my kids, the woman I had helped financially and emotionally through her divorce was having an affair with my husband. She had been giving him the sex he had told me a year before that he would no longer push me for. He wasn't going to push me because he knew where he was going to find it. And she knew too. I remember asking her long before he asked me for a divorce, "Do you think he has another woman?" Her response, of course, was no. So the betrayal was not just of the marriage bond; it was a betrayal of a close friend.

Seeing Beyond the Pain

Monique turned to the only source of help and hope she had known in life. She turned to God.

> My story could be one of betrayal and abandonment, but through Jesus Christ and His shed blood on the cross, I know that this story of mine is about hope, faith, renewal of spirit, and of the goodness of our Lord and Savior. And only the love that He gives to us is eternal. His love will not betray and will not abandon. He is steadfast when our world is turbulent and when those around us fail and are given to sin and hate.

Even when things went from bad to worse, Monique held on to God and His promises in the Bible. She clung to God's truth and took the high road of integrity even when she received threatening faxes, even when hateful untruths were circulated about her at work, even when sexually explicit messages and notes were left on her voice mail or in her office, even when details of her intimate life were retold in twisted ways to those she was supposed to manage.

You will feel better if you act in such a way that you are proud of the woman who looks back at you in the mirror each morning.

The desire for revenge and retaliation is natural under these unfair and unjust conditions. But that isn't taking the high road. You will feel better if you act in such a way that you are proud of the woman who looks back at you in the mirror each morning. Take the high road.

Monique took the high road when her husband drove a forklift through a wall at the company in anger. She took the high road when the majority of the employees turned against her because her husband promised them money. She took the high road when a group of her husband's buddies tried to steal office equipment, and the police had to come and draw their weapons. Even when her company was torn from her leadership, when her former husband sabotaged accounts and engineered a walkout for three days, costing the company approximately $50,000, she still took the high road and clung to truth like a lifeline of hope.

She decided she would walk through these dark days according to God's plan and His priorities. She decided to reflect on His character rather than seek revenge or retaliation:

> I firmly believe that God sustained me through it all, as I will call on Him to do again and again for the rest of my life and for the life of my children. I have had a spiritual journey of unbelievable depth. It still blows me away to know how good God is to His children. By taking the high road, the road that God calls us to, life is better and His sense of peace and contentment can be ours as followers of Christ.

Seeing the Fruit

Monique couldn't see the future God had planned for her, but she kept stepping out with integrity. She and her support group prayed for God's perspective and power before the myriad court appearances for both custody hearings and property and business hearings. "Lord, let the truth be brought to light," they prayed. "Shed your light of truth in the courtroom today."

> When you gain God's perspective, He gives you the ability to hear the applause from heaven.

In the end, though the business was taken out of her hands, the court awarded her a full salary and benefits, allowing her to be a full-time mom. She was given a fair settlement that paid for her return to college and a new home for her children. Because she maintained her integrity and grew so much in her relationship with God, a large church in the area hired her for ministry.

When you gain God's perspective, He gives you the ability to hear the applause from heaven.

When You Want a Pound of Flesh, Pray for Perspective

It's easy to want to take revenge on those who wound us. Unfortunately, when we act on those feelings, we pay the price the victimizer should have paid.

Ask Elisabeth "Betty" Broderick, whose story was made into a Lifetime Television movie. Betty was a devoted wife who set aside her career aspirations to help put her Harvard-educated husband, Dan, through law school. She then raised the children while he built a multimillion dollar legal practice in La Jolla, California. Later, Betty learned Dan had an ongoing affair with Linda, one of his employees, and she felt tossed aside when he divorced her to marry this younger woman.

Ed Whitney, an insurance agent who served with Elisabeth on

the court-watching group Help Abolish Legal Tyranny, remembered how Betty stood before their group and described in detail how she felt Daniel Broderick had used his legal influence in the court system to beat her in the divorce.

"She mentioned the original court date," Whitney said. "That Dan showed up in court, and that the judge said, 'Good morning, Mr. Broderick. To what do we owe this honor?'"[4]

Frustrated with the legal system, one November night in 1989, Betty used a key to gain entry into Dan and Linda's home and shot the couple as they slept. Betty now serves a life sentence for a double homicide. Though she had a right to be angry about the injustice she received, her unwise quest for revenge caused Dan and Linda to lose their lives, the four Broderick children to lose both parents, and Betty to lose her freedom.

When you take revenge, you pay the penalty that belongs to the offender.

When I work with women going through an unfair divorce or the trauma of a spouse's infidelity, I will sometimes hear, "I want to kill him!" Walk that choice out. He did the cheating and stealing, but you're the one who would end up in jail if you attempt to act on those feelings. Make the offender pay for his or her misdeeds by *not* taking revenge. God says, "Vengeance is Mine," and though it may take time to see His justice at work, it will come. People tire of toxic individuals, so eventually the person who wounded you will pay a price.

No one gains when a heart is run by revenge and anger. To temper your temper, I suggest you pray Scripture that asks God to intervene on your behalf:

> Do not take revenge, my friends, but leave room for God's
> wrath, for it is written: "It is mine to avenge; I will repay,"

> No one gains when a heart is run by revenge and anger.

says the LORD. On the contrary: "If your enemy is hungry, feed him; if he is thirsty, give him something to drink. In doing this, you will heap burning coals on his head." Do not be overcome by evil, but overcome evil with good (Romans 12:19-21).

GOD'S POWER

Walk in Power

Finally, the third tool that energizes your adventure when life is tough is *God's power*. Daniel 11:32 says that those who know their God will be strong and do mighty deeds. You are able to accomplish things way beyond your fear barrier.

God's adventure is worth fighting for, but fight for it God's way with God's tools in God's timing.

My friend Debbie was willing to do just that when her husband was stationed in Bahrain. When she told me this story, I said, "You are the most courageous woman I know!" And she said, "I simply believed God would be who He said He was and acted on it." Debbie was so hungry for God she was willing to risk, to dig deeper into who Jesus is. This is her story in her words:

My family and I moved from Germany to Bahrain in the Middle East. At that time, the base in Bahrain was under high security alert 24 hours a day. My husband was in charge of water and food inspection sites that supported our ships at sea, so he was one of a handful who had a "causeway pass" that allowed him to cross over the 12-mile stretch into Saudi Arabia.

I had the opportunity to go across with him on several occasions, the only military wife in Bahrain who had that privilege. However, I had to be very careful at the checkpoint to wear the appropriate black abaya and not to carry anything in my purse that would show I'm a Christian. I was also not allowed to carry any magazines or wear or carry makeup, or the border guards would confiscate it immediately. The guards, depending on their moods, would take hours to go over a vehicle piece by piece looking for western or Christian contraband. I felt spiritually dry and running on empty in this environment that offered so little spiritual growth opportunities.

I received a letter from my best friend, reminding me of a military women's retreat that was coming up in three weeks in Germany. My soul longed for spiritual enrichment, but I questioned myself, wondering how I could possibly get there. I mentioned this to my husband, and he said, "Maybe you can go on a military airlift flight." (The military provides available free space to dependents, retirees, and active-duty members.)

I was so excited that I immediately visited the American Embassy in Bahrain, hoping they would help me get an entry and exit visa. To my surprise, the Embassy had no authority beyond issuing the standard one entry and one exit pass per year for Saudi Arabia. For this trip, I would need an additional entry pass because I had already used my one entry visa the day we arrived in Bahrain. I prayed constantly for wisdom about what to do and how I could get to Germany.

One day I looked down at my Bible and a verse stood out in 3-D: "In the same way, faith by itself, if it is not accompanied by action, is dead" (James 2:17). That was my answer! I needed to step out in faith and get to Germany. Faith is a verb. Faith is action.

The only available military flights were out of Saudi Arabia. Since my husband had a "causeway pass," I hoped he could get me across to the airport in Saudi Arabia.

I called the airport and talked to a gentleman who sounded as if he was from India. I told him that I wanted to fly out on a MAC to Germany. When he asked if I had an exit and entry visa, I told him I only had one left.

"There is no way you can go," he said. "No way. It won't work. If you try to leave without both visas, you will be caught and go to jail until all the details are worked out, and that could take time. You cannot go."

"OK." I hung up the phone and thought, *That's his opinion. I am going one way or another. Faith is action.*

The next day I called the airport again and talked to the same gentleman.

"Are you Muslim?" I asked him boldly.

"No, I am not Muslim."

"What is your faith?"

He didn't answer.

"I'm a Christian woman and I must get to Germany, and you have to help me."

"Remember what I told you yesterday?" he said. "You will go to jail if you are caught, and you will be caught."

"I know, I know, but I need help! Can you please somehow, someway, get me on that plane that's leaving in four days?"

After a long pause, he said, "All right, I will put your name on the list. But you have to understand how dangerous this is. How will I know it's you when you arrive at the airport?"

"Well, it won't be hard to find me. I'm blonde and over six feet tall. Finding me in the airport will not be complicated. But how will I find you?"

"I will be behind the counter, and you will just know that it is me," he said. "Be careful." And he hung up the phone.

I immediately began to pray, *Lord, if you want me to get to the retreat, I need to see a miracle. I am scared to death. Really scared.*

To my surprise, the miracle was already in progress. My husband was very supportive of me trying to get on the plane. I was surprised that he was so willing to jeopardize his life and career for me.

I tried to pack as light as possible. I dare not bring my Bible, and it was hard to leave without it since the Bible is where I go when I need courage—and I needed courage!

At the first checkpoint on our way to the airport, the guard motioned us through. He didn't even have us stop. We came to the second checkpoint, and once again, the soldier motioned us through. We made it through all of the checkpoints without anyone checking my passport, suitcase, or purse. Miracle #1 complete!

When we arrived at the airport, my husband came in with me so the guards could see that I had a husband and was not a fleeing wife. (This is a common occurrence in Saudi Arabia, I was told.)

I waited in line trying to see behind the counter and guess which man I had spoken with on the phone. Finally, after waiting for what seemed to be forever, I was at the counter.

"Are you Mrs. Anderson?" the man behind the counter asked me.

"Yes, I am Mrs. Anderson."

He pointed to the other side of the room. "Go get in the other line. You are all checked in."

Yes! This was the man I spoke with on the phone. I never showed him my passport. The second miracle!

I said goodbye to my husband, and he whispered, "You'll be OK. I love you." And then he left.

I felt so alone and began to question myself. *What am I doing? Is it worth the risk?* I began to feel queasy and to wonder what would happen if I were caught.

A soldier who was headed home stood in the same line with me. I leaned over and asked him if I could pretend to be his wife. He laughed and said, "Okay."

It seemed as if I waited in line the longest I ever had in my life. I just wanted to get on that airplane.

Three Arab guards waited at the front of the line. I started to think I would have to show my passport, and they would see that I did not have an entry visa stamp. With only two people in front of me, the man at the counter who helped me earlier walked over and said, "We need to get this line moving!" And the guards waved me and several people through. The third miracle!

I now faced one final checkpoint at the top of the stairs entering the plane. My hands began to sweat and I felt sick to my stomach, but I kept telling myself, *Faith is action…faith is action.*

I headed up the stairs, and I could see the two guards at the top looking very stern. I prayed, *Please, Lord, please help me through this*. As I neared the top of the stairs and was about to extend my hand with my papers, I could hear a man behind us causing a commotion and running up the stairs. When he got to the top he said, "She's fine. Come on…let's get the people through." The fourth miracle!

I made it to Germany and the retreat. My story spread all over the conference center. The conference was just as renewing and encouraging to my soul as I knew it would be. But I still had to get back home, and I wasn't sure how that was going to happen. So all my friends there prayed for a miracle.

And the fifth and final miracle soon came.

I stayed on the Air Force base with my best friend for a few days after the conference. The one and only day I went to the air base to see if there were any flights to Saudi Arabia, I was told there were none, only one flight leaving that day to Bahrain. I could not believe what was said. *Bahrain*—my present assigned country and where my family was waiting for me. Unbelievable! Even the woman who worked at the counter mentioned how rare it was to see a flight to Bahrain.

So I did not have to worry about going through Saudi Arabia after all. I didn't need an entry visa. God was sending me directly home with my passport to Bahrain.[5]

When you need power, then pray powerful prayers from the Word:

His wisdom is profound, his power is vast. Who has resisted him and come out unscathed? He moves mountains without their knowing it and overturns them in his anger. He shakes the earth from its place and makes its pillars tremble. He speaks to the sun and it does not shine; he seals off the light of the stars. He alone stretches out the heavens and treads on the waves of the sea. He is the Maker of the Bear and Orion, the Pleiades and the constellations of the south. He performs wonders that

cannot be fathomed, miracles that cannot be counted…
He unleashes his lightning beneath the whole heaven and
sends it to the ends of the earth. After that comes the
sound of his roar; he thunders with his majestic voice.
When his voice resounds, he holds nothing back. God's
voice thunders in marvelous ways; he does great things
beyond our understanding (Job 9:4-10; 37:3-5).

God's dreams, God's plans are worth being prepared for and
will be achieved with His power, perspective, and peace. God's
adventure is worth fighting for, but fight for it God's way with God's
tools in God's timing.

Winning Words

Sing to the Lord a new song, for he has done marvelous
things; his right hand and his holy arm have worked salvation for him. But thanks be to God! He gives us the victory
through our Lord Jesus Christ…for everyone born of God
overcomes the world. This is the victory that has overcome
the world, even our faith…When I consider your heavens,
the work of your fingers, the moon and the stars, which
you have set in place, what is man that you are mindful
of him, the son of man that you care for him? You made
him a little lower than the heavenly beings and crowned
him with glory and honor. The heavens declare the glory
of God; the skies proclaim the work of his hands.

Winning Wisdom

Is there someone in your life who has hurt you, held you back,
betrayed you? It's natural to want revenge, but God asks us to place
the situation in His hands. Only by handing the battle over to the
Lord will you be free to go forward in life. If you keep mulling over
that injustice, betrayal, and hurt, you're handing over control of your
life to the very person who hurt you.

Ask God to give you perspective in those tight places. Ask Him for wisdom and clarity. Give control of your life back over to God and allow Him to fight the battle for you today. Gain perspective by focusing on a positive goal and do *something* today to take a step toward it.

WINNING WAYS

With your adventure team or fine-tuning friends, ask these questions:

- Which of the three ways to walk out your faith—walk in peace, walk in perspective, walk in power—will help you be fully convinced that Jesus is taking care of all you have deposited with Him?

- What did you learn in this chapter that will help you move your adventure forward when you feel under attack?

- This chapter has examples of several courageous women who faced some tough obstacles. Who did you most relate to: Monique, Debbie, or Pam? Why? What did you learn from her?

Remember these simple words of wisdom when you are ticked off by a trial or a person:

- "You cannot get ahead while you are getting even."— Dick Armey

- "Live well. It is the greatest revenge."—The Talmud

Even better, see if you or your team can come up with your own bumper sticker to remind yourself to pursue God's peace, God's power, and God's perspective when things get tough.

Managing Your Creativity

It's All About Energy

"You pay God a compliment by asking great things of Him."

TERESA OF ÁVILA

have been referring to your adventure throughout this book. This adventure exists because God is a creative God and He has placed a part of that creativity in you. You have the ability to imagine ideas, goals, and plans that work together to form a dream of what God might do during your days on the earth. This creativity is both fun and frustrating. It's fun because it adds dignity and hope to your life. It's frustrating because it constantly pushes you forward, demands your attention, and drives you to accomplish just a little bit more.

To stay creative, therefore, you need energy and enthusiasm. In a world that takes and takes and takes, you need to learn the art of God-centered replenishment. You've probably heard that one of the keys to success is time management. But Jim Loehr and Tony Schwartz, in *The Power of Full Engagement*, contend it is how we manage our *energy* that matters. I couldn't agree more. How we manage our basic resources of time, creativity,

> To stay creative you need energy and enthusiasm.

energy, and integrity determines our productivity and success in life and relationships.

THE ENERGY SOURCE

In Luke 2:52, our Savior models how to keep our energy level high in the pursuit of our dream: "And Jesus grew in wisdom and stature, and in favor with God and men." Let's break this verse down:

> Jesus grew in wisdom (guarded His intellectual life)
> and stature (guarded His physical life)
> and in favor with God (guarded His spiritual life)
> and men (guarded His social life)[1]

Let's look at how to guard our creativity, strength, energy, and potential by guarding these four areas of our lives.

HOW *WISE* ARE YOU?

Okay, I am blonde, and my whole life I've been fighting the misconceptions about deficient intellect that come with my hair color. I've heard most of the jokes, including this one:

> Q: Why do blondes always smile during lightning storms?
>
> A: They think their picture is being taken.

But I don't buy into all that "blondes are dumb" logic. I think more blondes are like this woman:

> A blonde walks into a bank in New York City and asks for the loan officer. She says she's going to Europe on business for two weeks and needs to borrow $5,000. The bank officer says the bank will need some kind of security for the loan, so the blonde hands over the keys to a new Mercedes-Benz SL550. The car is parked on the street in front of the bank.

She has the title, and everything checks out. The bank agrees to accept the car as collateral for the loan. The bank's president and its officers all enjoy a good laugh at the blonde for using a $100,000 Benz as collateral against a $5,000 loan. An employee of the bank drives the Benz into the bank's underground garage and parks it there.

Two weeks later, the blonde returns. She repays the $5,000 and the interest, which comes to $15.41.

"Miss, we're very happy to have had your business," the loan officer says, "and this transaction has worked out nicely. But we're a little puzzled. While you were away, we checked you out and found that you're a multimillionaire. What puzzles us is why you would bother to borrow $5,000."

The blonde replies, "Where else in New York City can I park my car for two weeks for only $15.41 and expect it to be there when I return?"

That's a new spin on blonde! And new is what spawns creativity. To be creative, to have new ideas, concepts, and notions run through my mind, I find it helpful to try new things, go new places, learn new principles, navigate new experiences, and meet new people. I like to picture my life like double-stick tape—everywhere I travel, every person I meet, every word I hear or read sticks to my life.

Pause here and ask yourself:

- Have I met anyone new this week?

- Have I eaten anything different?

- Have I traveled or visited a new place this month?

- Have I learned a new bit of knowledge today?

- Have I tried to gain a new skill?

- Have I cultivated a new talent?

- Have I tweaked something old to make it new (a room, a piece of clothing, an item of décor)?

- Have I exposed my mind to a new concept, new author, new musician, or even a new television or radio program?

Make a decision to do *something* new today. Write your goal for new living here:

My life has been enriched and enhanced by the itinerant ministry God has given me. People and places are interesting. Some people, ideas, memories, and experiences I've had are timeless, so I want them with me always. By synthesizing those ideas, new ideas of my own develop.

Ideas are fluid. They morph a little as they pass from life to life. Ideas are a little like the seeds in those dandelion puffs—some need to travel into a new environment to be cultivated and developed by the person God entrusts with the stewardship. However, I don't want *every* idea or experience to stick to me or my life. Some ideas and experiences are rooted in things that oppose God. I want to pick off those things from my double-stick tape and flick them into the gutter.

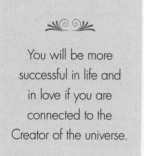

You will be more successful in life and in love if you are connected to the Creator of the universe.

We each need a grid by which we judge all beliefs, concepts, people, and experiences. This grid functions much like the strainer you use to drain your pasta. The pasta stays, but the unwanted water drains through the grid. The good and godly ideas stay; the destructive and toxic thoughts drain away.

In this book I've made a clear contention that you will be more successful in life and in love if you are connected to the Creator of the universe. Let me share how my connection was strengthened and how my belief grid developed.

A Reliable Grid

Just as a diamond has many facets, so does my belief in God. To guard my intellectual life, I had to go on a journey of intellectual integrity to check out the facts from many different points of view. First, I needed to check out the book that holds the story of God: the Bible. I knew that many books claim to contain sacred writings, but I wanted to see which one was the most reliable historically, logically, and philosophically. I looked at all the world's main religions (and most so-called cults). I read about their founders, the main tenets of their beliefs, and where those beliefs would lead if you followed them.

After this in-depth journey I concluded that all the belief systems, except one, were about man trying to reach God. If we are good enough, pious enough, and devoted enough, then maybe we might somehow be fortunate enough to be invited into glory (heaven, nirvana, and so on).

The biggest flaw with these belief systems is man's big flaw: imperfection. We are simply *not* devoted enough, pious enough, or good enough. In a word, we fail...consistently. (If we think we're pious enough, then we are proud, which amounts to another failure!) One failure, one shortcoming, one flaw is enough to ruin our chances. With world religions there is just no guarantee of the "happily ever after," let alone a future of hope here on earth. Only one religion, Christianity, has God reaching down to man and providing a solution to man's big dilemma of imperfection. Jesus, who was and is God, came down and died on the cross, sacrificing Himself to pay the penalty of our imperfection.

Only a perfect, eternal being can offer the eternal sacrifice needed to pay the penalty for our imperfection (or what the Bible calls sin). As the apostle Paul says, "God made him who had no sin [Jesus] to be sin for us, so that in him we might become the righteousness of God" (2 Corinthians 5:21).

I became even more confident when I realized the Bible could be scrutinized by external methods and stand up to every test. The Bible has been proved reliable every time it is examined through the lenses of history, eyewitness accounts, writings of those from that time period and soon after, and archaeology. Because it is beyond the scope of this book to explore this question in depth, I recommend a book I used to traverse this territory (*Evidence That Demands a Verdict* by Josh McDowell) and a few written since my journey (*The Case for Christ* and *The Case for Faith* by Lee Strobel and *Taking a Stand for the Bible* by John Ankerberg and Dillon Burroughs). In these books you'll discover overwhelming evidence for the reliability of the Bible and all its claims.

Ours is not a blind faith. Ours is not a faith based on feelings or conjecture. No, ours is an intellectually sound faith based on reason, based on evidence.

What concerns me today is how few people take the time to think through the foundations of their lives. Some simply believe as their parents believe (which can be good if you've talked through the issues with your parents and have owned your own faith). Others just go with whatever is popular or trendy. This means the media or your social circle is leading you. Most people simply don't give much thought to the deeper issues of life. There is a prevalent and global "whatever" attitude, a kind of "all roads lead to the same place" philosophy that puts all beliefs at the same level of intellectual security.

While I am a huge proponent of freedom of speech and religion, this doesn't mean all philosophies are equally sound. They can't be since many of them contradict one another.

Guarding your mind guards your spiritual destiny. God has already extended an invitation to you, but if you do not choose Him, you send yourself to an eternity of darkness. It is not a party in hell; it is complete and utter aloneness forever. If we believe that, then we must share the hope that is within us. Sharing the hope of a personal relationship with God is, or should be, at the core of every Christian's adventure, whether the adventure is personal or professional, a ministry or a business, a hobby or an organization. The desire to glorify God and make Him known needs to have some place in the adventure, even if it's simply a commitment on your part to engage in a healthy, holy lifestyle.

> Laying a strong foundation for your adventure is essential for life's success.

I encourage you to think and pray through your life's foundations because the process will help you gain the ability to reason, to plan long term, to see ahead of time the consequences of your choices. The ability to be a reasonable, thinking person who does her "due diligence" and research on all decisions will serve you well on your path to your dreams.

Ask any of the followers of David Koresh, Charles Manson, Jim Jones—oh yeah, you can't ask them. They're dead or in jail because their decision to follow blindly led them to destruction.

Become a thinker. I know many of you are much more intellectual than I am, but you may not have stopped long enough to become a thinker about what really matters most—your eternal destiny.

It's okay to push *pause* and develop your ability to think and reason. Take an apologetics class, go through a video series such as *The Truth Project*, read a book by Josh McDowell, Lee Strobel, John Ankerberg, J.P. Moreland, Nancy Pearcey, or Lael Arrington. Pick up an audio book or attend a lecture that stretches your mind. Laying a strong foundation for your adventure is essential for life's success.

How *Strong* Are You?

If anyone understands how hard it is to stay in physical shape, it would be me. I was a college athlete, then taught gymnastics for years, only to begin writing…and my battle of the bulge. I know I'm not alone in this struggle, as indicated by a recent bumper sticker I saw:

> Inside me there's a thin person struggling to get out,
> but I can usually sedate her with four or five cupcakes.

Nonetheless, I keep working at it because physical strength promotes emotional wellness, mental alertness and creativity, and spiritual obedience. God tells me my body is His temple. In guarding my physical life, I guard my creativity.

I'm guessing a few of you are like me and need a little motivation to break a sweat. Treadmill tests conducted on people between the ages of 12 and 49 found that about one out of every five had poor cardiovascular fitness, including about one-third of the teenagers and one out of seven young adults.[2] In a recent poll of more than 1,400 people, just over half said they were generally satisfied with the amount of exercise they get. But federal health statistics show that most Americans aren't getting very much. Two-thirds are not physically active on a regular basis and a quarter get practically no exercise at all.[3]

> The majority of us who care about reaching our God-given dream are a bit out of shape.

So it's probably true that the majority of us who care about reaching our God-given dream are a bit out of shape. Can I motivate you (and me) a little then to get active by reminding you of the benefits of physical activity and fitness? The list is impressive:

- Being alive (It's much easier to achieve your adventure this way!)

- Release of endorphins, which lift your mood

- Shapely appearance (It boosts your confidence and makes swimsuit season less traumatic.)

- Sexual interest (For our married sisters—you might appreciate this, but your husband will appreciate your renewed interest even more.)

- Strength to achieve the adventure (You sleep better, can work longer, and travel stronger.)

- More money (Less money is spent on medicines, insurance rates, or health aids.)

- More time (Being sick is time consuming and can be a distraction from adventure achievement.)

- Easier breathing (More oxygen means more brain power, which can protect creativity and learning.)

- Higher productivity

- Flexibility (Tasks are easier and less painful.)

- Lower stress (Experience fewer headaches, less anxiety, and more overall enjoyment of life.)

- Friendships (Many physical activities are done in groups so you might also enhance your social life.)

Move for a Creative Breakthrough

In an analysis of over 200 studies, periodic aerobic exercise was found to have a short-term positive impact on creativity, but daily exercise that leads to long-term fitness has the most positive impact. One study found that creativity increased in generally fit individuals immediately after exercise because there was more oxygen available to the brain.[4] Generally unfit individuals didn't get the same immediate benefit. Scientists thought it could be due to the body using all its energy to recover from the exercise. So sign up for an aerobics class, go for a run, or swing your partner do-si-do and get that mental breakthrough you desire!

Mediocre Is Not an Option

One of my heroes in health is my long-time friend Debbie. We became friends in college, and she was there during my days of dating Bill and was a bridesmaid at our wedding. By watching Debbie, I have seen the courage that an active lifestyle produces.

My husband once said, "I'd like to see Debbie at a dinner party when someone does the 'Well, that's nothing. I...' bragging moment. We could just let Debbie share her adventures, and she'd win!"

Here are a few of the adventures Debbie has navigated: She was one of the first women hired to fight forest and wildfires for the California Fire Department. She became one of their first captains. She has hiked the Grand Canyon rim to rim and to the top of Yosemite's Half Dome alone. She biked across Europe several times. She has led seven trips to Russia to help with church planting and women's ministry. She has kayaked the Colorado River through the Grand Canyon, the length of the Baja Peninsula (on the Gulf of California side), more than 1,000 miles on the Yukon River, and around Patagonia, the southernmost part of South America. She took a ferry to Seward, Alaska, and then paddled back to Juneau on the open sea to her home on the backside of a glacier. In 2007 she was named the top outdoor educator in Alaska and was selected to lead the Discovery Channel team as they filmed their Alaskan specials. She is currently the director of women's ministry at her church. With her active lifestyle she guards her creativity physically; with her mind she guards her creativity intellectually; with her heart for serving God she guards her creativity spiritually and socially.

What was the seed of her courage, confidence, and creativity?

The Seeds of Creativity

In college we attended a leadership conference together from which she came away with a couple of life mottos: "Know where you are going and who you are taking with you," and "I *never* wanted to live the mediocre life." Her life has been anything but mediocre.

She has set her sights on traveling to every continent (including Antarctica) before the age of 50. Debbie's life has been, and still is, filled with excitement, activity, and adventure. She is one of my heroes because she has demonstrated what can happen when you commit to an active lifestyle. She has lived her dream.

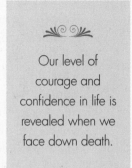

Our level of courage and confidence in life is revealed when we face down death.

I asked her once how she, a single woman, has been brave enough to do so many of these danger-filled adventures alone. "Well, if I died I would just go to heaven a little sooner," she said. "I prepare well, then trust the outcome to God. I know where I'm going." Only a woman who has guarded her life socially, spiritually, physically, and intellectually can make a bold, courageous statement like that.

Our level of courage and confidence in life is revealed when we face down death. While we might not need to strap ourselves into a kayak to do it, we will all benefit by coming to grips with the fact we are all terminal. All of us will die someday. It's what we do with the days between now and then that matters. Those are the days of living the adventure.

When walking out the adventure of your life, make it your goal to take as many as you can with you so on that eventual day when you step across heaven's threshold, you will hear "Well done."

How *Spiritual* Are You?

Spiritual creativity is cultivated in our daily dialogues with God. I can't tell you how many great ideas for work, for relationships, for success in my physical, social, or spiritual life have come during or just after my times of prayer or Bible study. It's as if my relationship with God sweeps out the negative, the superfluous, the menial, and the mundane, and in their place He adds His wisdom, His insights, His creative juices. Ideas that are better, bigger, and bolder appear.

King Solomon, the leader called the wisest in the Bible, explained this correlation to his son:

> For the LORD grants wisdom!
>   From his mouth come knowledge and
>   understanding.
> He grants a treasure of common sense to the honest.
>   He is a shield to those who walk with integrity.
> He guards the paths of the just
>   and protects those who are faithful to him.
> Then you will understand what is right, just, and fair,
>   and you will find the right way to go.
> For wisdom will enter your heart,
>   and knowledge will fill you with joy.
> Wise choices will watch over you.
>   Understanding will keep you safe.
>
> (Proverbs 2:6-11 NLT)

When I have a mental block or face an emotional curveball, a physical challenge, or a spiritual attack, I take time to push *pause* and pray. I read the Word and I pray. I pray before I panic. I pray before I press forward. I pray before I pursue my own agenda.

Satan doesn't want you to succeed. He wants to steal your creativity and hijack your life.

My prayers often are not long or profound. Sometimes they are well worded, written out as if they are a love letter to Jesus from my heart. But more often my prayers are my heart's cry, "Help! I need You! Can You give me something—anything—here? Pleeaassse!"

Our lives are a battleground. Satan doesn't want you to succeed. He wants to steal your creativity and hijack your life. To paddle through the treacherous waters you may encounter, it's wise to have a plan in place. Our difficulties define us.

Handling Relationship Crises

We have talked much about handling trials along the adventure. However, we haven't delved into how to handle the hard relationship issues that might sidetrack our adventure or turn it into a nightmare. In a nutshell, here are some simple steps I encourage people to take when faced with a crisis in their marriage or family (and the steps work pretty well for most any kind of trauma).[5]

Name It. Acknowledge that a situation is presenting itself. Say something like, "We have a situation on our hands. Can we pray?" Don't hide your head in the sand or pretend that it isn't happening. That usually just compounds the situation. If someone else names it for you, don't be offended. Listen and seek a third opinion. If someone notes that your marriage seems strained or your child seems troubled, test it by asking your sounding-board friends their opinion or seeking professional help.

Resource It. Find out as much as you can about what you're dealing with. Read up on it, google it, find the professionals best equipped to help you. Ask around to see if others in your social circle or church have had to deal with it too.

Staff It. Often the help you need is multifaceted. Seek out a physician, a psychiatrist, a counselor, or friends and mentors who have navigated something similar. Look for support groups steeped in handling whatever issue you find yourself needing to navigate. Look for the best professional in every field to be a part of the team.

Plan for It. When dealing with crisis, break it into two pieces: the emergency plan (the next 24 to 72 hours) and the long-term plan. Call your team together to help you create and implement the emergency plan. Once your situation has stabilized, reconvene with the team to help you create the long-term plan for moving from crisis to creativity.

Pray over It. Put together your prayer team. Call your best friends together for a prayer time. Prayer walk with a friend. Put yourself on the church prayer list if you're comfortable with the crisis being made public. Use a concordance or biblegateway.com to look up verses on the topic you're dealing with. Begin to pray the verses over your life and family.

When my husband experienced a health crisis that affected ministry and finances, I prayed verses of God's goodness, anointing, and favor over Bill, our kids, our ministry. I told my friends and family, "Let's give God time to be good. Somehow He will show His character and rescue." I prayed Job 42 over Bill that God would give him "double for his trouble," as Joyce Meyer puts it. I prayed that Bill's influence, our finances, and our opportunities would double. Within a year we saw those requests answered and more.

Vacation from It. Sometimes you just need to push *pause* and get away from it all. When you're away and can think from a more rested and relaxed position, new insights or new appreciation of your loved ones surface. When a couple is in marriage crisis, we often suggest they take the money they would spend on lawyers and take a vacation to Hawaii or Europe instead. Being away together often helps them rediscover their love so that they don't need to call the lawyers when they return. If a child is in crisis, sometimes time away with you will provide an emotional breakthrough for them.

Look beyond It. Keep your eye on the goal. You will not always be in this pain. The storm will pass or you will adjust to what my friend Carol Kent calls "a new kind of normal" (also the title of her recent book). You will laugh again, and there will be reasons to celebrate. You will once again feel whole and hopeful.

Team Up on It. Make a conscious choice to not take out your emotions in a negative way on your spouse, children, parents, and friends. It's important to share your feelings, but try to do it in a calm, honest way. Blaming and angry outbursts will just compound the crisis.

Redeem It. By taking your eyes off yourself, you can turn your pain into a passion to help others. John Walsh, the host on *America's Most Wanted*, never wanted his young son, Adam, to be stolen and killed. But John has used his pain to save hundreds of missing children and change laws to make the world a safer place. Candy Lightner founded Mothers Against Drunk Driving (MADD) after her daughter, Cari, was killed by a repeat drunk driving offender. Cindy Lamb, whose daughter, Laura, became the nation's youngest quadriplegic at the hands of a drunk driver, soon joined Candy in her crusade to save lives. These moms didn't ask for the trauma, but they did redeem it to save the lives of others.

HOW SOCIAL ARE YOU?

Newspapers in major markets usually contain a society section. In some cities, country clubs and philanthropic organizations host balls and galas to raise money for worthy causes. Black-tie dinners with $5,000-a-plate tickets mark the social calendars of the elite. These often feature worthy causes and noble adventures.

However, I look elsewhere for inspiration to help me decide how to spend my time, talent, and treasure socially. I was moved by the story of a mother who walked the African desert barefoot to look for her children stolen by rebels to serve in a bloody war over earthly riches. Mother Teresa won the Nobel Peace Prize for serving in the slums of India. Linda Smith rescues women and children from sex slavery. Anabel has lived her entire life ministering in war-torn East Timor.

> When strength, spirituality, wisdom, and social justice come together, lives change.

If I am involved on some level with social justice, I am motivated for all of life. When my social life makes the world a better place, that is truly fulfilling. When my relationships are on solid ground, I am stronger and more confident, and so are the people I'm relating to.

When strength, spirituality, wisdom, and social justice come together, lives change. Change agents often come in unusual packages. Adventure launches from unusual places when God is in charge. Take, for example, the social and spiritual influence of Sojourner Truth, a former slave. Historian Mary Arnold says of her, "She was a dramatic and inspirational speaker leaving audiences filled with emotion. The simplicity of her language and the sincerity of her message, combined with the courage of her convictions, made Sojourner a sought-after speaker."

In 1851, Frances Gage, an abolitionist and president of the Women's Rights Convention, captured one of those moments in her report on the proceedings of a convention held in Akron, Ohio:

> Sojourner walked to the podium and slowly took off her sunbonnet. Her six-foot frame towered over the audience. She began to speak in her deep, resonant voice: "Well, children, where there is so much racket, there must be something out of kilter, I think between the Negroes of the South and the women of the North—all talking about rights—the white men will be in a fix pretty soon. But what's all this talking about?"
>
> Sojourner pointed to one of the ministers. "That man over there says that women need to be helped into carriages, and lifted over ditches, and to have the best place everywhere. Nobody helps me any best place. And ain't I a woman?"
>
> Sojourner raised herself to her full height. "Look at me! Look at my arm." She bared her right arm and flexed her powerful muscles. "I have plowed, I have planted, and I have gathered into barns. And no man could head me. And ain't I a woman?
>
> "I could work as much, and eat as much as a man—when I could get it—and bear the lash as well! And ain't I a woman? I have borne children and seen most of them sold into slavery, and when I cried out with a mother's grief, none but Jesus heard me. And ain't I a woman?"
>
> The women in the audience began to cheer wildly.
>
> She pointed to another minister. "He talks about this thing in the head. What's that they call it?"

"Intellect," whispered a woman nearby.

"That's it, honey. What's intellect got to do with women's rights or black folks' rights? If my cup won't hold but a pint and yours holds a quart, wouldn't you be mean not to let me have my little half-measure full?

"That little man in black there! He says women can't have as much rights as men. 'Cause Christ wasn't a woman." She stood with outstretched arms and eyes of fire. "Where did your Christ come from?

"Where did your Christ come from?" she thundered again. "From God and a woman! Man had nothing to do with him!" The entire church now roared with deafening applause.

"If the first woman God ever made was strong enough to turn the world upside down all alone, these women together ought to be able to turn it back and get it right-side up again."[6]

Out of the Shackles

Sojourner Truth was born Isabella (Belle) Baumfree, the child of slaves. Sold numerous times, she grew to womanhood as a slave. Sojourner became a very strong woman, both mentally and physically, during her years of bondage. Through her beatings, she learned determination. As was true of many slaves, Sojourner lost her parents and was forbidden to see the man she loved. She dealt with her pain privately, and as she was taught in her early childhood, she put away the hurt when it was time to work. Her owner, John Dumont, made her marry a slave named Thomas. Together they had five children, and her cruel owner sold most of them. Sojourner had heard about God from her mother, and she prayed to Him every day for relief from her bondage.

Two years before Dumont was legally obligated to set Sojourner free, he approached her with a proposition. He promised her that if she worked extra hard for him over the following year, he would set her free one year early. Wanting freedom and wanting to believe in the integrity of her owner, Sojourner agreed and put in endless hours of grueling work. But Dumont broke his promise.

Deeper In, Higher Up

Sojourner cried out to God, begging Him to help her escape, and the Lord spoke to her. He told her to set out several hours before daylight and directed her late the next night to a Quaker home, where she was given shelter.[7]

When Sojourner won her freedom in 1828 under the New York State Anti-slavery Act, she encountered God again.

> An' says I, "O God, I didn't know as you was so great! An' I turned right around an' come into the house, an' set down in my room; for 't was God all around me. I could feel it burnin,' burnin,' burnin' all around me, an' goin' through me! I saw I was so wicked, it seemed as if it would burn me up. An' I said, "O somebody, somebody, stand between God an' me for it burns me." Then, honey, I said so, I felt as it were somethin' like an ambrill [umbrella]— somebody that stood between me an' the light, an' I felt it was SOMEBODY—somebody that stood between me an' God; an' it felt cool, like shade; an' says I, "Who's this that stands between me an' God? Who is this?"...I began to feel 't was somebody that loved me; an' I tried to know him...An' finally somethin' spoke out in me an' said, THIS IS JESUS! An' I spoke out with all my might, an' says I, "THIS IS JESUS! Glory be to God!" An' then the whole world grew bright, an' I said "Praise, praise, praise the Lord!" An' I begun to feel such a love in my soul as I never felt before—love to all creatures.[8]

Sojourner Truth became a famous preacher, speaking out for women's rights and abolition, but mostly she preached a living gospel that drew people to a personal relationship with Jesus Christ.

Sojourner didn't let her humble beginning, her gender, or her former slave status hold her back from speaking out. She knew her potential came from being a redeemed woman with a passion to spread the same message of hope, help, and redemption she had experienced. Creativity was God's gift to free her to bring about sweeping social change in a bankrupt culture.

Free to Reach God's Potential

We all have chains of lies and half-truths that shackle us, robbing us of achievement, blocking us from arriving at our full potential. When we first step out on our path to adventure, it is easy to feel insignificant. Most people, when they feel belittled or marginalized, also feel stifled creatively.

A budding author I was mentoring came back from a writers' conference completely deflated. One person's comments to her served as a roadblock to her writing. She felt paralyzed. She is one of the most talented writers and leaders I know, but because of the stinging words, she was like an airplane in a stall pattern, spiraling down. She called me in tears. "I thought I was reading God right—that He wanted me to write—but the editor said, 'Who are you?' meaning I don't have a big platform or an impressive bio. Pam, he actually said, 'Who do you think you are? You are nobody.'"

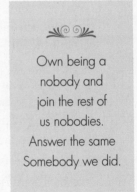

Own being a nobody and join the rest of us nobodies. Answer the same Somebody we did.

I was outraged on her behalf. "You are not nobody," I said. "You are somebody. You are the same somebody as any of us with platforms and bios were when we first began. At the starting line, we are all nobodies! God is the only somebody, really. And when He calls, since He is Somebody, we answer the call."

Own being a nobody and join the rest of us nobodies. Answer the same Somebody we did. Let God build the platform, the bio, the reputation as He did for any of us who are walking the adventure.

It would have been easy for me to believe the lie that I was a nobody and had nothing to offer. Children who grow up in homes with alcoholism and rage often struggle with low self-esteem and a lack of confidence. But I was introduced to the Somebody who makes every nobody a somebody with an important adventure to discover and live out. Live God's adventure creatively, and you will be energized for life every day.

Ready to paddle the adventure?

Winning Words

Righting wrongs is energizing. Pray these verses over areas of life you feel passionate about:

> For the Lord loves the just and will not forsake his faithful ones. They will be protected forever. The King is mighty, he loves justice. Do not follow the crowd in doing wrong. Good will come to him who is generous and lends freely, who conducts his affairs with justice. The righteous care about justice for the poor, but the wicked have no such concern.
>
> Learn to do right! Seek justice, encourage the oppressed. Defend the cause of the fatherless, plead the case of the widow. Let him who boasts boast about this: that he understands and knows me, that I am the Lord, who exercises kindness, justice and righteousness on earth, for in these I delight.

Winning Wisdom

> Jesus grew in wisdom (guarded His intellectual life)
> and stature (guarded His physical life)
> and in favor with God (guarded His spiritual life)
> and men (guarded His social life)

Which area of your life needs attention to follow Christ's model? If we are to follow in the Lord's footsteps, we should not look at the steps but at the Person making the prints.

Charles Price's mentor in ministry was John Hunter, one of Britain's leading evangelists who was known for preaching hope and peace and for the saying, "For this I have Jesus." One day Charles heard that John had suffered two successive strokes, and so he called to offer his love and prayers. John Hunter's wife told Charles she wasn't sure how much her husband would be able to communicate, but knowing he would be delighted to hear from Charles, she held the phone up to her husband.

"For this I have Jesus."

"I am so sorry you are going through this difficulty," Charles said.

Through slurred speech, Pastor Hunter replied, "For this I have Jesus."

For this I have Jesus. That one line of hope has been repeated in the face of tragedy, crisis, and stress. When life feels out of your control, remember that it's not out of God's control. The same Jesus who said to the waves, "Be still," can calm the waters of your life, but more important, He can give you peace in the midst of the storm. For this you have Jesus.

How well do you know Jesus? Do you have verses memorized that show His character, that give you a glimpse of His majesty? In the Gospel of John, Jesus gives many word pictures describing who He is. These metaphors can give you peace and strength in the midst of the storms of life.

- Jesus is the Word—When you need clarification, wisdom, discernment, then look to the ultimate guide (John 1:1).

- He is the light—When you need guidance, look to Him for your next step (John 1:4; 8:12; 9:5).

- He is the bread of life—When you feel empty inside, look to Him for fulfillment (John 6:35,41,48,51).

- Jesus is from above—When you need perspective, look to Him and ask to see life from His vantage point (John 8:23-24; 12:32).

- Jesus is the Son of Man; He is truly human, sympathetic to our frailties, and yet He is perfect—When you're feeling fragile, fallible, and frail, look to your sympathetic Lord for aid (John 8:28).

- Jesus is the gate for the sheep—When you need a place of safety, go to Him and you'll find rest (John 10:7,14).

- Jesus is God's Son—When you need power beyond your own to cope with life, take your concern to Him (John 10:36).

- Jesus is the resurrection—If you feel hopeless, despondent, or frustrated, look to the one who raised Himself from the grave to raise you up and give you hope and help (John 11:25).

- Jesus is the true vine—We must be connected to Him for nourishment (John 15:1).

- Jesus is king—When you need to appeal to a higher power, a greater authority, appeal to Jesus who reigns in majesty (John 18:37).

- Jesus is the living water—When you are thirsty for something to quell the longings, to handle the cravings that seem to overpower you, then look to Jesus, and His presence will bring refreshment (John 4:10).

- Jesus is God—When you need forgiveness, grace, mercy, and a fresh start, come to the Author of life (John 13:19; 14:11,20; 18:8).

If you've never read through the Gospels of Matthew, Mark, Luke, and John, begin today. In your journal, record any verses that help you gain a clearer picture of Christ and give you strength for your journey. Then you too can grow in wisdom, stature, and favor with God and man.

Winning Ways

With our energy and creativity we can make a difference in this world. As an adventure team, make a list of ten injustices in our world today and begin praying about what God would have you do to reflect His holy and just character in at least one of those areas. Then discuss these questions:

What keeps me insulated from the pains and ills of society?

What can I do to build a bridge to keep in tune with the plight of injustice? Volunteer with a people-helping organization? Make a friend of a different socioeconomic level? Tutor? Mentor? If you already have such a relationship, do something that expresses how you value that relationship.

Ask God to reveal to you ways you might act unjustly or in an unholy way. Then ask Him to show you a better way to respond that more closely reflects His character.

Talk about how other-centered your adventure is. Are you like Debbie who wants to live more than a mediocre life? Or Sojourner, the "nobody" who led many others to the great Somebody? Or have you been selfish with your adventure, thinking it existed for your pleasure and your purposes?

Are you stuck in a rut? Since new people and experiences help cultivate creativity, share with your adventure team that one new thing you will try this week.

How are you managing your energy? If we want to live the dream in a way that lasts, we need to pay attention to all four areas (intellectual, physical, spiritual, social).

We all have the same amount of time. How are you spending yours to maximize your energy and impact in this world? What goals or lifestyle changes do you need to make to ensure your energy is maximized? Share your goals with your adventure team and hold each other accountable for movement in those energy-building areas. Someone's future may depend on how well you manage your creative energy.

STEP into God's Adventure

Speak the Adventure
Team up for the Adventure
Energize the Adventure
Push the Adventure

Forge Forward

The Adventure in Focus

*"Reach high, for the stars
lie hidden in your soul. Dream deep,
for every dream precedes the goal."*

PAMELA VAULL STARR

elen Duff Baugh was a woman of focus. Raised by parents with a strong faith, she grew up understanding that prayer, Bible reading, and evangelism were part of everyday life. Her mother was a talented Bible teacher and evangelist, and her father trained hundreds to be ministers on every continent.

In the early 1900s, Helen's family decided to move from Ireland to America. Her father, Reverend Walter Duff, came to the states ahead of the family, and then he booked passage for the rest of them on the safest vessel of the day—the *Titanic*. However, Helen's mother, Mathilda, missed her husband so desperately that she changed the travel arrangements, and the family set sail two weeks earlier than originally planned. Helen, though just a child, couldn't help but notice the providence of God when she heard the newspaper boy shout, "Extra! Extra! *Titanic* Sinks!"

When Helen was 12, she came to know God in a personal way and began to sense His hand in her life. In her autobiography, *The Story Goes On*, she writes:

While still in my teens I remember a community called Park Place near us where a lovely church was standing vacant, and I asked Father if we could start a Sunday school there. Father agreed, and we went to check on the use of the building. As we discussed this with various people in the community, someone said, "Why not let them go ahead? They are only young people and they can't do any harm." So we started calling in every home in the community. Everyone was invited to Sunday school, and soon we had the place filled, not only with children but adults as well.[1]

This was just the beginning of Helen's ministry, a ministry that called her to rural communities that had church buildings in need of repair and people in need of leadership. Helen describes one church that stood out in her memory as "very dilapidated…the windows were all broken out, the door hanging open, and strange to say, the big pulpit Bible was lying open on the pulpit, its pages flipping back and forth in the wind." Helen was haunted by the picture of churches across the country in this neglected state and towns vacant of the vital living hope of the gospel.

Soon the Duff sisters found themselves traveling through rural America, singing and planting Sunday schools, leading vacation Bible schools, and engaging in other creative works. These pursuits often helped to strengthen a small, weary congregation that longed for the quality teaching and leadership the girls provided. Many times their ministry resulted in a new congregation that continued after they left.

The girls soon married. Helen wed Elwood Baugh, a successful executive who had a big heart and loved to use his talents and resources to serve God and others. Helen enjoyed domestic life in San Jose, California, but longed to do something eternally focused to bring Christ to her community. She began to pray with a new friend, the city manager's wife, and soon a prayer meeting developed every Monday morning. While driving through a different neighborhood, she began to pray for this area of her community as well. Soon she met a woman in the area and started a prayer meeting there on Monday afternoons. She contacted another friend in a different part of town, and a Tuesday group developed. Then Helen was asked to come to her husband's bank on Wednesdays to lead a prayer meeting for any employees who wanted to pray during lunch.

Soon 24 groups were meeting for prayer on different days of the week.

> She longed to do something eternally focused to bring Christ to her community.

One evening, Helen's husband told her that some of the single women at his bank had many questions about God and hoped he could answer them. Elwood saw this as a wonderful opportunity for Helen to minister to the women, and so the Baughs treated the women to dinner out while they answered their questions. It went so well that the women wanted to meet again the next week.

The meetings quickly became more formal, and the women decided to name the organization the Christian Businesswomen's Council. The Baughs encouraged the group to take on a ministry project—and what better project than rural American churches. Soon the ministry duplicated itself in other cities, and each of these groups committed to funding a team of young women ministering in a rural area.

REGROUPING FOR THE ADVENTURE

One day Helen traveled with her children to Cannon Beach, Oregon, to visit a ministry team there, leaving her husband at home to work. While she was at a dinner with her extended family, there was a knock on the door. It was a Western Union messenger with a telegram telling Helen that Elwood had been killed in an accident.

Helen was shocked and grief-stricken. Elwood had been the

love of her life and her partner in the vision. What was she to do now? In desperation, she picked up the daily devotional she and Elwood had been reading. On the day of his passing, the Scripture read, "When thou goest, thy way shall be opened up before thee step by step." It was as if God had sent a personal message of hope, and a strange sense of peace enveloped Helen. She didn't know exactly how it was going to work out, but she knew God was calling her forward.

Helen accepted that God had a plan for her without Elwood, and in time, her grieving was replaced with a new focus. She courageously committed to step into a life of purpose—a life with her eyes off herself—as the leader of this new organization. It was going to take more focus than she had ever experienced, but she knew that God was faithful.

The work of the Christian Businesswomen's Council grew. Soon Helen's sister, Evangeline, and her husband, Archie McNeill, formed a new organization called Village Missions to provide leadership for rural churches. Both organizations grew rapidly. The Christian Businesswomen's Council expanded to include other professional women and also helped the work of Village Missions by supporting the organization financially.

To maintain focus, the first step is to make sure sights are clear.

When many of the young professional women got married, they decided to form a new group in order to reach their friends with the good news of Jesus. As a result, Christian Women's Clubs were born. Husbands, too, wanted to use the same outreach-oriented format to reach couples, and soon several Professional Couples' Clubs were formed. Coffees for follow-up and discipleship naturally followed. All these outreach ministries needed booklets and other written materials, and so a publishing company sprang up to meet the need.

This burgeoning ministry needed a permanent home, and as in all decisions, Helen committed the need to prayer. She and her team decided to ask the Lord to provide the money for the need. They were led to Stonecroft, a lovely country home on many acres outside Kansas City. When the papers were signed, the ministry agreed to pay at least $200 a month. Helen writes:

> From the very inception of this ministry, it was my policy that I would not send out letters asking for money…We did let people know that we had bought the property and told them that only gifts earmarked for the purchase would be used that way. Soon the gifts began to arrive…It was time to make our first payment…so down to the bank went our bookkeeper with the checks. After handing the [bank officer] a check for $200 for the first payment, [our bookkeeper] said, "We'd like to give you this, too." And she handed the man a check for $2,000!

The next month was the same—$200 with $2,000 extra. So the bank sent out a representative to ask the ministry to *slow down* repaying the loan.

MAINTAINING FOCUS

Focus is necessary to forge forward. To maintain focus, the first step is to make sure sights are clear. When I go to the optometrist, she gives me a test and asks a set of questions: "Is it clearer like this, (flip the lens) or like this?" We go through a set of lenses to determine which ones will give me the clearest vision. When I am formatting the adventure, I compare my thoughts with a checklist I developed through my experience and my study of Scripture to ensure my focus remains clear.

Before you decide something is God's dream for you, or when you need to refocus your future, run down the following checklist. (I'll first give you the list, and then we'll dive in together for more detail.)

TEN CS FOR CLARITY

- *Counsel:* Have I asked God for guidance from His Word to lead me or confirm His will?

- *Confidants:* Have I gathered mentors and friends who love me and love God's Word and asked them to be my sounding board?

- *Confirmation* of the Holy Spirit: When I picture myself living this decision, do I see the fruit of the Spirit at work in me?

- *Concurrence:* Is God repeating Himself? Am I getting the same message from many different directions and sources?

- *Cooperation:* Am I already doing what I know is God's will so I can be lined up to receive His next directive?

- *Calendar:* Have I asked, "Is this the right season for me, my family, or my organization to launch this dream and succeed?"

- *Community:* Do the people on my team (spouse, family, business partners, employees, boss, volunteers, teammates) buy in and believe in the dream?

- *Competency:* Is this dream reasonable for me, my life, and my organization?

- *Countdown:* Have I lined out the steps to achieve the dream? And have I followed the timeline backward to see if I have the people, finances, and time I need to do a quality job and succeed?

- *Circumstance:* Am I seeing God open doors yet?

DIGGING A LITTLE DEEPER

Counsel: I always ask God for a Scripture passage that speaks to my heart when I'm contemplating a dream or a decision. I place the verses that confirm my passion, dream, or call in the flyleaf of my

Bible so that when times get tough, I can flip open my Bible and say, "Yes, this might be hard, but here is evidence of a clear call." (As a reminder that this is a good idea, read Psalm 119 and note all the benefits of walking in the Word.)

Confidants: When you are at a fork in the road, consult your adventure team, your mentors, and your friends and family to get their opinions of the plan and how you are interpreting God's path. Use them for a sounding board. You want people who love you, believe in you, love God, and love to see people walk in God's path. This gives them the right attitude and the ability to speak truth (sometimes hard truth) to you, or speak encouragement in a way you can receive it. Proverbs 11:14 says, "Where there is no guidance the people fall, but in abundance of counselors there is victory" (NASB). By reading this book with some girlfriends, you can begin to build your prayer and advisory team if you haven't already.

Confirmation of the Holy Spirit: As you step out into the decision, the fruit of the Spirit should become evident ("But the fruit of the Spirit is love, joy, peace, patience, kindness, goodness, faithfulness, gentleness and self-control"—Galatians 5:22-23).

When Israel crossed the Jordan River to enter the Promised Land, the water didn't part until the priests, who were leading the procession, put their feet into the stream. Sometimes you will be anxious about a decision, but as you step into it and walk it out, you should begin to see all the fruit of the Spirit at work. If not, recheck the decision.

When Bill and I were deciding whether to marry, we chose to take the summer apart and not communicate by phone or letter (there was no texting or e-mail then). We would just pray and see what God told us.

Before Bill went home to work for the summer, he stopped by my place. We prayed together, and then he got in his car and drove south. All the way he felt God impress on him that he was to marry me. But then he would argue, "God, I can't marry Pam. I'm only twenty years old. I haven't finished my degree." When he'd argue with God, his stomach would knot up and he'd be anxious, and so he'd give in and say, "OK, God, I'll marry the girl." Then he'd get peace.

Then he'd argue with God again. "I can't marry. I don't have a real job. I work part-time at a gas station. I own only two pairs of pants and one has a rip in the knee. I drive a blue Vega with a green back door." He'd argue and he'd be tied in knots, so he'd surrender and say, "OK, I'll marry the girl!" And he'd get peace.

Then he'd argue once more. "God, I can't marry. I want to be in ministry. If I marry I'll never finish college, let alone seminary. I know how this works—we marry too young, we never finish college, and we end up broke, resentful, and miserable." Bill would be all tied up in knots, and then he said in finality, "OK, fine! I'll marry the girl!"

So OK, fine! He married me and he's had peace. Peace comes as we step out into the dream…if it's God's dream.

Concurrence: In Scripture, when something is important to God, He repeats it. I think that is how He works in our lives too. If God is trying to get our attention, He will send the message through a Scripture, a sermon, a conversation with a friend, a story a stranger tells us, a radio or TV program. He will bombard our life until we get it!

One day I was getting the kids ready for school, and a guest on *Family Life Today* was talking about how to handle anger. On the way to school, I heard James Dobson interview a guest on *Focus on the Family* about how to handle mommy anger. When I got home, I turned on the TV and Kay Arthur was preaching on "Don't let the sun go down on your anger…" I went to the mailbox, and my copy of *Today's Christian Woman* magazine was there with an article on handling anger.

Then I picked up my children from school, and we began our after-school homework routine. We had a two-story home, and we had a rule not to yell from upstairs if you needed someone. You were to walk down and ask quietly. That day the boys yelled down at me, and I stood at the bottom of the stairs and screamed, "You boys know the rule! If you want something, walk down these stairs and get me!" My little toddler, Caleb, tugged at my pant leg. "Mommy, I don't think God likes it when you yell at us."

Wham! The Holy Spirit nailed me! God repeated the message loud and clear, "Deal with your anger." I immediately went to the Word to find the solution to pull out the root of anger. (Which, by the way, was a series of exercises designed to kill the control freak in me. I began to study the sovereignty of God—which led me to study the traits of God, and all that research led to this book! I don't have to be in control when I'm resting in God's ability to be in control. This has led to a calmer, nicer, less-controlling mom.)

I don't have to be in control when I'm resting in God's ability to be in control.

Cooperation: To be in line for your next set of marching orders from God, you need to be waiting and working in the plan He has revealed to you already. Elisabeth Elliot, wife of martyred missionary Jim Elliot, told how she decided to stay and work among the same indigenous tribe that had murdered her husband. She said, "I did the next thing." Even if you don't know the whole path, ask God to show you just the next step. Then do the next step. God can steer a moving ship.

The next step in cooperation is to live a yielded life. Walk in a blameless, holy, teachable way. There are benefits to integrity. Underline the word or phrase in each passage that explains a perk of integrity:

- Do good, O LORD, to those who are good, to those who are upright in heart (Psalm 125:4).
- My shield is God Most High, who saves the upright in heart (Psalm 7:10).

- LORD, who may dwell in your sanctuary? Who may live on your holy hill? He whose walk is blameless and who does what is righteous, who speaks the truth from his heart (Psalm. 15:1-2).

- May integrity and uprightness protect me, because my hope is in you (Psalm 25:21).

- Vindicate me, O LORD, for I have led a blameless life; I have trusted in the LORD without wavering (Psalm 26:1).

- In my integrity you uphold me and set me in your presence forever (Psalm 41:12).

- He holds victory in store for the upright, he is a shield to those whose walk is blameless, for he guards the course of the just and protects the way of his faithful ones (Proverbs 2:7-8).

- The man of integrity walks securely, but he who takes crooked paths will be found out (Proverbs 10:9).

- The integrity of the upright guides them, but the unfaithful are destroyed by their duplicity (Proverbs 11:3).

These are just a few of the verses from Psalms and Proverbs. There are more! It seems integrity guides you, helps you be secure, puts you in a place where God shields you, stores up wisdom for you, keeps you in God's presence, redeems you, places grace on you, vindicates you, preserves and saves you, and allows you to live in God's tent. Sounds like a pretty great way to live to me.

Calendar: Set a start date for your adventure. Then list out all the steps needed to work out the details of the dream and place those details on a timeline. Have you allowed enough time for successful achievement of the dream? Have you calculated in a margin to overcome unseen obstacles? Have you factored in that some on your team might not work with the same fervor, passion, and dedication, making their pace slower than yours? Set a reasonable pace so you can enjoy the path of your journey.

Have you checked the season of life you are in? Can your marriage handle the changing obligations and pressure of a new dream? Can your children handle the change? What will be the domino effect in your private world and in your personal relationships?

In a marriage and family cycle, there are seasons that have a high learning curve (newlywed, newly parents, parents of preschoolers, parents of teens, married to a midlife man or woman in crisis, caring for aging parents). This doesn't mean that dreams cannot be launched in these seasons, but you should realize that there will be a lot going on in your personal world already, so weigh out the decisions and timeline carefully. Launching new dreams is a little easier in certain seasons: after you have been married a year or few, after you have a couple of children, after the kids are all in school, after the children leave home. These are all natural times of transition, and the time clock God planted in you will be ringing, "Try something new!" Because of this, you will have more natural energy and motivation.

Community: You will want your team to have buy in. We discussed this in detail in earlier chapters, but it's good to pause here and ask, "Can the people in my world handle this adventure?" If you have a high-needs child, you might have to locate some caregivers first. If you have a rebellious teen, you might need to postpone your dream until you help your child through the struggle. If you have a husband in his own transition (new job, demanding project, midlife crisis), you might need to walk the adventure at a slower pace to make room to minister to your spouse.

Sometimes I have been right on track in my timing, but a couple times I have jumped the gun. When I get ahead of God, the people around me get overstressed, and so do I. We might make it through, and the project or decision might be achieved, but it isn't as much fun! Instead of elation at the finish line, it's more like stumbling across the tape and collapsing in a heap.

Competency: Can you and your team handle this adventure? For example, if I told you I was planning to become a college math professor, you would likely laugh out loud if you knew me. I got a D in high school geometry; I had to have Bill tutor me through college math courses. I hate handling finances and accounting. Teaching math is just not a realistic dream for me. Not impossible, but probably not the best use of my time and talent.

> Make room for growth in your own abilities and the skills of your team.

However, if I said I wanted to teach college English, no one would blink an eye with my resume of straight A's in English and communication classes and 26 books under my belt, a couple of them bestsellers. I might have to polish up my grammar and review some classroom techniques, but the learning curve would not be nearly as steep.

In your pursuit, make room for growth in your own abilities and the skills of your team. When you decide to walk out the adventure, pause and ask, "If I'm not competent already, what will it take? How much time? Money? Energy? Who will need to be on my team: mentors, family, friends? And what will I need to ask them to do for me? Is the team surrounding me competent to handle this decision or dream? Do they need more training, education, equipping? Do I need more education, training, resourcing? Do I need to add new teammates with skills in this area? Is this dream the best use of my time, talent, and treasure?"

Countdown: You will want to count the costs. Jesus told us that we should be like architects and figure out what it will take to complete a project. "'Suppose one of you wants to build a tower. Will he not first sit down and estimate the cost to see if he has enough money to complete it?'" (Luke 14:28). When you plan and prepare, you build confidence because you can picture success.

I placed this verse on my personal stationery:

The Sovereign LORD is my strength;
he makes my feet like the feet of a deer,
he enables me to go on the heights.

(Habakkuk 3:19)

God knows the plans He has for me that will lift me to the heights (successes) He has designed uniquely for me. God has the ability to communicate the dream to me and the strength to secure it.

You also want to count the loss. To be ready to step out, you have to picture what would happen if you risk and it doesn't turn out the way you envision. The verse from Habakkuk quoted above is preceded by a reminder of the necessity of trusting God when things don't go according to plan.

When you realize you can lose everything except your faith and rise out of the ashes, you are ready to walk God's adventure.

Though the fig tree does not bud
and there are no grapes on the vines,
though the olive crop fails
and the fields produce no food,
though there are no sheep in the pen
and no cattle in the stalls,
yet I will rejoice in the LORD,
I will be joyful in God my Savior.

(Habakkuk 3:17-18)

So if the worst happens—the adventure falters, you fall flat on your face, the bank account is empty, and life turns inside out and backward—and yet you still know God will be there for you, then you are ready to step into the adventure He has for you. When you realize you can lose everything except your faith and rise out of the ashes, you are ready to walk God's adventure.

Circumstance: Eventually God will open the door. Sometimes He delays so we can gain the character we need to live out the call on the other side of the door. Other times He blows open the door so we see it's a miracle only He could have done, and He alone gets the glory and credit. One way or another, if you've walked through this checklist and know your adventure is God's will, the doors will start to open. You might have to push on some of them, but God will move on your behalf if this is His adventure for you.

Any woman who wants to fulfill God's purpose in her life must make a commitment to maintain focus.

When God opens the door, you'll know it because your attitude will show it. You will know it was *not you* but *Him*.

Several places in Scripture show the thrill that comes when God answers: Midlife Miriam picked up a tambourine and led the women in dance after God brought Israel through the Red Sea; Mary sang the Magnificat when she realized she was to give birth to the Messiah; David danced before the Lord when he brought the ark of the covenant into Jerusalem; 45 years after the Lord promised Caleb an inheritance in Canaan, his dream was accomplished. That must have been a party day!

KEEPING IN FOCUS

Focus is the ability to stick to a task regardless of the distractions. Focus clears a path where there has been none. Focus provides the fortitude to hang tough, to push through, to come back to the main thing and keep it the main thing. Focus is what keeps us on task and prevents our lives from drifting to mediocrity.

Any woman who wants to fulfill God's purpose in her life must make a commitment to maintain focus.

Helen Duff Baugh knew what focus was. She was able to carry out God's unique calling in her life because she maintained focus on His purpose for her throughout her life. The ministry that began in her youth blossomed into an organization called Stonecroft Ministries, which now includes over a thousand staff members and spans a number of diverse ministries. As a result of Helen's focus, thousands of other people have discovered their God-given ministries. That's the way focus works. When you stay focused on God's calling, you enable others to discover their calling as well.

Any woman who wants to fulfill God's purpose must make a commitment to maintain focus. The everyday demands of life will try to steal your ability to focus. Life's setbacks will try to discourage you from completing the plan God created uniquely for you. To get to the finish line of God's purpose for your life, you must have a plan to keep your desire high. I recommend the following ways to maintain focus.

Look to the eternal. I have come to realize that life is longer than 70 or 80 years. It is eternal. Most of my life will take place in the presence of God, and nothing on earth can take that away from me. The important part of my life, then, is the investment I make in eternity. With this in mind, I often ask myself, *Is what I'm doing today making an investment in eternity?* When I have to choose between two pressing needs, I ask, "Which has a more eternal focus?" Seeing life from this perspective enables me to keep my heart focused. Our friend, Ken Nichols, has a ministry whose name, ALIVE Ministries, reminds me of how to live daily: **A**lways **L**iving **I**n **V**iew of **E**ternity.[2]

> If we focus on our shortcomings or setbacks, we guarantee failure. If we focus on God's plan, we will fulfill His purpose.

Look to the reward. Everyone will work harder if they know there is a reward. Ultimately our reward comes in eternity. God speaks much of these rewards: "And when the Chief Shepherd appears, you will receive the crown of glory that will never fade away" (1 Peter 5:4). Eternal rewards await.

However, it also helps to have smaller rewards along the way. A massage, a day off, a movie, a date with Bill, fun with my three boys or a friend can keep me in focus. A smaller reward reminds me of the bigger reward to come.

Look to the goal. If we focus on our shortcomings or setbacks, we guarantee failure. If we focus on God's plan, we will fulfill His purpose. Keeping my goals in focus is a tough challenge, so I will often review the goals I have set and why they were important to me at the time. A short memory is the enemy of long-term goals! I post my goals in Outlook, write them on a whiteboard in my office, place them on 3 x 5 cards to review whenever I'm waiting in an office or in line.

Prayer elevates me to a heavenly perspective and provides the desire and strength to see the vision become reality.

I like to buy items to remind me of my most important goals. One of my associates recently bought me a music box that plays the same theme as a conference series I'm launching. As I sit in my office and the workload mounts, a look at the music box will remind me of all the women who will be blessed by the work.

Look to fine-tuning friends. God has faithfully put people in my life who believe in my adventure. They are not blind to my shortcomings, but they are highly supportive of God's calling in my life. Sometimes I have to ask them to help me say no to a good thing that will be a distraction for me. They encourage me through prayer, phone calls, e-mail, and face-to-face conversations. When I feel myself losing focus, I look to them for help. That is what the *Winning Ways* activities are all about in this book.

Look to the promise. To be honest, sometimes the need to keep our word gives us the ability to hang in there. We made a promise and we want to keep it. We want our reputation to be, "She comes through. We can count on her." Forging forward to maintain your

honor, your integrity, and your word is noble, and in a world of little follow-through, someone who keeps her word is refreshing.

Look to prayer. More than anything else, prayer keeps my heart focused. Prayer elevates me to a heavenly perspective and provides the desire and strength to see the vision become reality. The more in tune I am with God—the more I communicate with Him—the more I am able to focus. And through prayer, God communicates to me the purpose He has for my life.

But sometimes we cannot hear God speaking to us. I believe Dallas Willard, in his book *Hearing God,* captures the true problem people face when they feel they are not hearing from God: "Perhaps we do not hear the voice of God because we do not expect it. Then again, perhaps we do not expect it because we know that we fully intend to run our lives on our own and have never seriously considered anything else." [3]

How easily we forget that "in him we live and move and have our being" (Acts 17:28). Willard continues, "Generally speaking, God will not compete for our attention…God will not run over us. We must be open to the possibility of God's addressing us in whatever way he chooses, or else we might walk right past a burning bush instead of saying as Moses did, 'I must turn aside and look at this great sight, and see why the bush is not burned up' (Ex. 3:3)." [4]

We are not required to manufacture our own purposes. We are called simply to listen to the calling of God.

Sometimes, though, we think we hear God, but because we are human, imperfect, fallible, we may not always hear or receive the message well. Joyce Huggett, a missionary and Christian author, gives this advice, "If you believe God has told you to do something, ask him to confirm it to you three times: through his Word, through circumstances, and through other people who may know nothing of the situation."

As we grow in faith, God enables us to discern His voice more clearly. And when we cry out with a desire to live a life reflecting His character and calling, He answers. The Book of Proverbs tells us:

> and if you call out for insight
>   and cry aloud for understanding,
> and if you look for it as for silver
>   and search for it as for hidden treasure,
> then you will understand the fear of the LORD
>   and find the knowledge of God.
> For the LORD gives wisdom,
>   and from his mouth come knowledge and
>   understanding.
>
> (Proverbs 2:3-6)

> Trust in the LORD with all your heart
>   and lean not on your own understanding;
> in all your ways acknowledge him,
>   and he will make your paths straight.
>
> (Proverbs 3:5-6)

When I am in need of direction and strength to maintain my focus, I like to pray. In this chapter's Winning Wisdom section, I give resources you can use to enrich your prayer life.

A LISTENING HEART

God clearly wants to communicate with you about His plan for your life. We are not required to manufacture our own purposes. We are called simply to listen to the calling of God.

And what is the result of a listening heart? Helen Duff Baugh could answer that. In an era when very few women led any organizations, she answered God's call to lead. Her focus led to Stonecroft Ministries, whose work reaches all 50 states and 61 foreign countries. Many women today are running businesses, organizations, and ministries that began with just a whisper of an idea and a mustard seed of faith.

One woman, with a heart for the unreached, listening to God's calling for her life can impact thousands of people. If you focus on God's calling today, what could God do through you?

While a guest on *The Hour of Power*, I saw the "Possibility Thinker's Creed" posted on the wall of the church Dr. Schuller founded: "When faced with a mountain, I will not quit! I will keep on striving until I climb over, find a pass through, tunnel underneath, or simply stay and turn that mountain into a gold mine with God's help."

My husband, Bill, daily prays with me and usually closes the prayer with, "God, do through us what is beyond us." Let God do through you what is way beyond your wisdom, strength, power, and creativity. Let Him into your life and dream. Focus on His will, and then hold on for the adventure of your life!

> 🐌 🌀 🐌
>
> "God, do through us what is beyond us."

WINNING WORDS

The key to success lies in Christ, the author of all dreams. Focus on Him as you pray these verses over your life, your adventure, and your adventure team:

> And everyone who calls on the name of the Lord will be saved. Salvation is found in no one else, for there is no other name under heaven given to men by which we must be saved. We believe it is through the grace of our Lord Jesus that we are saved. Since we have now been justified by his blood, how much more shall we be saved from God's wrath through him! For if, when we were God's enemies, we were reconciled to him through the death of his Son, how much more, having been reconciled, shall we be saved through his life! That if you confess with your

mouth, "Jesus is Lord," and believe in your heart that God raised him from the dead, you will be saved. For it is with your heart that you believe and are justified, and it is with your mouth that you confess and are saved. But I pray to you, O LORD, in the time of your favor; in your great love, O God, answer me with your sure salvation.

WINNING WISDOM

I like to use Scripture to enhance my prayer walk because the power is not in my words but in God's Word. I use resources such as:

- *My Personal Promise Bible for Women* (Honor Books) or *Daily Light on the Daily Path* (J Countryman Publishers)
- *Wives in Prayer* notebook (available at www.farrelcommunications.com)
- Scripture prayer cards from your local Christian bookstore
- Scripture calendars (A beautiful one with art from Timothy Botts is available at inkwellgreetings.com. There are several with inspirational quotes from women authors plus a daily Scripture. Check with your local Christian bookstore for options.)
- Scripture to music (like *Scripture Medleys* available at www.waterthroughtheword.com, or *Family Worship* from seedsmusic.com)

I also create my own prayer resource with a spiral set of 3 x 5 cards that you can get in any office supply store. I use this resource to record my favorite empowering verses. I then review them en route while walking, exercising, waiting, and traveling (by plane, not while I'm driving!).

I will often prayer walk with Bill or a friend and pray the verses aloud. Sometimes I will read and record the verses into my computer and create my own personalized podcast (I can even download it to my iPod) or use the memo feature on my phone and simply replay them as needed for encouragement. I also create a set of verses and pray them over my husband's, children's, and even some of my adventure team's dreams.

My friend Marcia Ramsland, author of *Simplify Your Time*, has a habit that has strengthened her life for years. In her planner each day she writes the verse from her quiet time that God gave to empower her life. Regularly she cuts the verses from her planner and puts them on a key chain chosen to represent that year. At the end of the year, she has a portable source of encouragement that she can carry in her purse or place on her nightstand for those times when she needs a boost of personalized TLC from God's Word.

Here is a sample of something you can record and play back for your own life:

> I call on you, O God, for you will answer me; give ear to me and hear my prayer. Hear my voice when I call, O LORD; be merciful to me and answer me. I will call upon you in the day of trouble; you will deliver me, and will honor me. But I call to God, and the LORD saves me. Then my enemies will turn back when I call for help. By this I will know that God is for me. If God is for me, who can be against me? From the ends of the earth I call to you, I call as my heart grows faint; lead me to the rock that is higher than I. You are forgiving and good, O LORD, abounding in love to all who call to you. Lord, you say, "He will call upon me, and I will answer him; I will be with him in trouble, I will deliver him and honor him." I call out to you; save me and I will keep your statutes. I call on the LORD in my distress, and he answers me. The LORD is near to all who call on him, to all who call on him in truth.

How can you layer more of God's Word into your life to sharpen your focus on the adventure He has for you? Select a method and invest in it this week.

Winning Ways

Acts 1:8 says, "But you will receive power when the Holy Spirit comes on you; and you will be my witnesses in Jerusalem, and in all Judea and Samaria, and to the ends of the earth." Your adventure might be in business, media, sports, relationships, or ministry. Whatever your adventure is, a part of it should be the desire to be a light to those around you. Jesus said we are a light to the world. The Spirit of God will empower you to reach your world with the hope and help of the good news of a personal relationship with Christ.

Who is in your world? Focus on these three circles:

1. *Your Jerusalem (your closest circle of friends and family).* In your journal, list five people you will begin to pray for that they might come to know God personally.

2. *Your Judea (your neighborhood, dorm, business circle).* Begin to pray that God would show you one effective way to share your faith with those you have something in common with.

3. *Your Samaria (those you have zero in common with, you don't like, or may even be afraid to be seen with).* Choose one people group that is hard for you to love and do something to help that group sense God's love for them. For example, give an at-risk kid a camp scholarship *and* take her to lunch, write her a note, or send a gift package to her at camp.

Share with your adventure team your answers to who is in each of these circles. Also tell them how you are going to invest in your prayer life through one of the resources in Winning Wisdom. Then talk about how your adventure, whatever it is, might best be used to be a light to the world and express God's goodness and greatness. How can achieving your adventure bring glory to God?

Practice giving God the glory for your success. Pray these verses with your adventure team or fine-tuning friends:

> In Christ Jesus, then, I have reason to be proud of my work for God (Romans 15:17 ESV). May I never boast except in the cross of our Lord Jesus Christ, through which the world has been crucified to me, and I to the world (Galatians 6:14). Let [me] rejoice and be glad and give him glory (Revelation 19:7). His divine power has given us everything we need for life and godliness through our knowledge of him who called us by his own glory and goodness (2 Peter 1:3). [I am] the light of the world…Let [my] light shine before men, that they may see [my] good deeds and praise [my] Father in heaven (Matthew 5:14-16). To him who is able to keep [me] from falling and to present [me] before his glorious presence without fault and with great joy (Jude 24). Therefore, as it is written: "Let him who boasts boast in the Lord" (1 Corinthians 1:31).

Endurance

She Who Hangs in the Longest Wins

"Far away, there in the sunshine, are
my highest aspirations. I may not reach them,
but I can look up and see their beauty, believe
in them, and try to follow where they lead."

LOUISA MAY ALCOTT

*I*t all began with a note:

> Please help this boy. His father is a drunk. His mother
> is a whore. Mother has left home; he needs help. Look at
> what his mother did to him.

Soon after reading these words, Grace and Steve Cabalka were
sitting in a Romanian orphanage, waiting to meet the little boy they
hoped to bring back to the United States for medical help and, if
possible, adoption. Grace writes of their first meeting:

> Mario came in and with barely an audible whisper said,
> "Bunazia" (good day), gave us a kiss and very meekly
> sat on Steve's lap. He stayed about an hour. That night
> I wrote in my journal, *Mario seems so sweet. His hair and
> complexion seem undernourished, his eyes look dull...as all
> the kids here do. They have no life, nothing to look forward to.
> I found myself reserved toward him because he is not released
> to us yet.* I had noticed that his clothes were three sizes

too small and dirty, that he had burn marks on his legs, and his left foot was turned out at a 90-degree angle. I remember noticing a patch of eyelashes was missing and there were several other scars as well. I wondered how long it would take him to heal from the emotional scars within.[1]

Grace and Steve believed that God had called them to adopt Mario and were aware that many challenges lay ahead of them. Their three other children would have to adjust to his presence in their home. People would ask them over and over again if they were sure about what they were doing. And there would be years of emotional and physical healing to endure. But the biggest challenge of all was working with the Romanian government.

At first Grace thought the process would be straightforward and relatively efficient. Their goal was to get everything done in two business days. "All we had left to do was go to court, get a birth certificate, get a passport, obtain a visa, get signatures of release from some authorities, buy airline tickets…and we had fourteen hours to do it!" Grace said.

We are often called by God to embark upon journeys that are fraught with numerous challenges and barriers.

What followed was two frenetic days of encountering repeated obstacles with the courts, the orphanage, the passport office, local bureaucracies, and even the airlines. Grace and Steve worked hard with the time they had available, but they also needed God to work for them, and they needed wisdom to know exactly what to do. Their efforts were interspersed with frequent heartfelt prayers imploring God to make a way. And in the end, God opened the right doors at just the right times, and they were able to take Mario home. Their lawyer proclaimed that what they accomplished was "beyond human power."

BREAKING BARRIERS

On your adventure journey, you will run into obstacles. There may be barriers that need to be broken. By consistently trusting God, Grace and Steve were able to stay on course. He gave them the strength and endurance to finish their journey, despite the obstacles that stood in their way. Like Grace and Steve, we, as women who dare to live out our adventure, are often called by God to embark upon journeys that are fraught with numerous challenges and barriers. But breaking barriers is not for the faint of heart or the uninformed.

When I need a model for forging ahead into hostile territory, I turn to John 4:6-42 and glean from Christ's interaction with the Samaritan woman at the well. In His decision to enter Samaria and talk with this woman, Jesus broke down some of the most formidable barriers of the day (and of our day as well).

Racial/ethnic barriers. During the time of Christ, Jews thought of Samaritans as second-class citizens, half-breeds, and apostates. If you were traveling from the Galilean region in the north (Nazareth, Cana, Capernaum) to Jerusalem in the south, the most direct route would be straight through Samaria. However, Jews would add another day of travel just to go around Samaria because they didn't want to tarnish themselves by coming in contact with this despised group of people. Jesus did not let this barrier deter Him from carrying out God's eternal plan to make disciples of all nations. Instead, He and His disciples went directly through Samaria and ministered to the people of that nation.

Gender barriers. During this time women were seen as property, and most women never had the opportunity for education. But Christ affirmed that women have equal value in God's eyes. He often engaged in teaching conversations with women, as He did with the Samaritan woman.

Class barriers. The woman at the well wasn't exactly the mayor of the community. She wasn't serving on the city council. She wasn't even prominent at the women's bridge club. She was going to get water at the well, doing servant's work. But Jesus did not think Himself above her; rather, He freely engaged her in conversation.

Piety barriers. Not only was the Samaritan woman doing servant work, she was not even a moral woman. She had had five husbands and was living with another man who was not her husband. She was looked down on by society, shunned by the mainstream social circle. She was likely pretty lonely, as most women wouldn't stoop to talk with her. She might have had male companionship, but with the kind of baggage she carried, she likely had some trust issues. She might have even felt alone in the company of the current man she was with. Christ knew all that, but He never shied away from sinful people.

The Samaritan woman lacked much in life, but she had what most people lack—a hunger and thirst for the truth. She longed for God and desired a relationship with Him (see John 4:15-28). She knew she had a need only God could fill, though she had tried everything else.

LET THE WALLS COME DOWN

Little by little, Jesus broke down the barriers between the Samaritan woman and Himself. But how? What steps did He take to overcome society's norms and reach out to the Samaritan people?

Build vision. Christ had an eternal mission, and people's agendas and politics were not part of it. Jesus had limited time on earth to carry out His task; He didn't have time to be sidetracked by the barrier that the Jewish society had constructed with the Samaritan people. Instead, He focused on the plan God the Father had for His life.

I have found that if I keep my focus on serving God, He will remove barriers in my life. I have been the first white woman speaker in some large

By keeping my eye on the eternal goal, the people who tell me I can't do something go out of focus.

African-American, Asian-American, and Hispanic churches not because I set out to do so, but because the message God asked me to share struck a common chord in those dedicated women. I have been asked to address male audiences, finding myself as the only "skirt" on the platform, not because I'm carrying a sign for gender equality, but because I have chosen to pick up my cross and follow Jesus. I serve on boards where I'm the only woman in a room full of men not because I'm engaged in any gender war, but because I'm concerned about winning hearts to God.

As we serve God, God will make a path for more service. By keeping my eye on the eternal goal, the people who tell me I can't do something go out of focus. I fix my eyes on Him who is the author and perfecter of my faith, and I see what I am called to do. As I do it, cultural barriers fall.

> We give people confidence when we walk just ahead of them and extend a hand of training out to them.

It is exciting to see gender barriers topple so women are free to say yes to service to God in whatever area of calling He has for them. But those barriers will continue to come down only if we keep our focus on the greater good, not our personal victory. An "I told you so" attitude will slam the door shut. We will gain more ground if we reflect Christ's mission and vision: "I seek not to please myself but him who sent me" (John 5:30).

Build relationships. Christ focused on building relationships with key people who had a heart for God. He poured His energies into building a community with His disciples. Because they knew Jesus was giving His all for them, they were loyal to Him—even when He endangered their reputations by taking them through places like Samaria. They followed Him even when He spelled out the cost, challenging them to "take up your cross and follow me." Eventually the relationship meant so much to those disciples they would give their life for the call.

Jesus didn't lead from an ivory tower. He led by walking just a step ahead. I am not a tall woman, so in crowds my husband will extend his hand to me. I will hold on to him and follow his broad shoulders as we swim upstream. I can't see the destination, but I can see him. In the same way, we give people confidence when we walk just ahead of them and extend a hand of training out to them. I never want to distance myself from those I am passing the torch to. At a leadership conference, I heard Howard Hendricks so aptly say, "He who calls himself a leader but has no followers is simply taking a walk!"

Jesus also knew that to reach the world, He had to reach the hearts of those closest to Him. He and His disciples ate together, traveled together, and ministered together in an effort to consistently strengthen their relationship.

Sometimes we can lose sight of people in the midst of running the program. I work at carving out one-to-one time with my team, using snatches of time to keep relationships strong. E-mails praising a job well done, phone calls of encouragement or concern, "thinking of you" notes scribbled on postcards from far away cities are a few of the small things I do to keep relationships growing amidst the frantic pace of leadership life.

Thanking the people who support us is another important part of building relationships. Every year for Thanksgiving, each person in our family gets to invite a family to our home for a Wednesday pre-Thanksgiving meal. At that dinner, we thank those families that have been an encouragement to us. We light a candle at each of their plates and give them a blessing, recognizing that our ability to accomplish our goals is directly related to their involvement and influence in our lives.

Build bridges. Christ sought to build bridges with the people around Him. He looked for the best, most fertile hearts, which often came packaged in the most unlikely persons. When we are seeking to create a path from one heart to another, from one thinking pattern to another, from one culture to another, we should seek to build a bridge.

Building bridges, however, is not an easy task. Most bridges of change are hard won, time consuming, energy intensive—and worth it!

How do you start? Look for a person who is also seeking to build a bridge. The woman at the well was looking for ways to worship God. When Christ offered her living water, she was eager to hear more of what Jesus had to say. Many of the strides in race relations are made because two people from opposing sides are seeking a common goal. They are looking to build a bridge to people who share the dream, regardless of ethnicity.

Look for common ground. Maybe you don't agree on everything, but what do you agree on? Build on those things. I serve on the board of several interdenominational organizations. We have the ability to pull people together from all kinds of backgrounds because, instead of traversing all kinds of theological trails that might lead to differences, we focus on the theological principles we all agree upon.

The strongest confidence comes when you know, moment by moment, you are in tune with God.

Jesus and the Samaritan woman didn't have a lot of common ground. The differences were enormous. He was a Jew; she a Samaritan. He was holy; she was wicked. He was a teacher; she was uneducated. At the time, He was respected; she was scorned. But Jesus was tired and thirsty, and the woman had a jug to draw water. The woman was thirsty spiritually, and Jesus could give her living water. By using water as the common ground, He drew the woman into a spiritual conversation.

From there He used the natural ebb and flow of a conversation to build a bridge between them. He didn't condemn her or focus on her shortcomings; He treated her with respect. He won over her heart, and she convinced everyone in her town to meet Jesus, the Messiah.

STEP-BY-STEP

Breaking down barriers by building vision, relationships, and bridges is a lifelong process, and more often than not, you will face resistance. You may have doubts within yourself, others may have doubts about what you are doing, and circumstances may be daunting. But if in your heart you know that the goals you are pursuing are what God designed you for, and your heart tells you to continue despite the obstacles, hang in there.

The strongest confidence comes when you know, moment by moment, you are in tune with God. And if you are His child, He lives in you through the person of the Holy Spirit. It is an awesome thing to have the Holy Spirit available to you and be able to rely on His help. But it does no good to have the resource if you don't have access to it. I loved God for years and unsuccessfully tried to follow His ways, but I didn't understand how to walk in the Spirit. It wasn't until someone explained Galatians 5:25 to me that I began to experience God's strength in my daily life: "Since we live by the Spirit, let us *keep in step* with the Spirit" (emphasis added).[2]

If I want to carry on a close conversation while walking with a friend, I must keep in step with my friend. If my friend turns, I must turn also. If there's a fork in the road, we have to take the same road or the conversation will be cut off. The same is true with the Holy Spirit. So my goal is to stay in step with the Holy Spirit. When you are in step with God's Spirit, your adventure will be easier to walk out because you will hear, step-by-step, what to do and say. God will fill you in on the details of the adventure as you walk with Him.

Every season of life requires endurance, and your ability to persevere increases exponentially when you walk in step with the Spirit. He gives me the endurance I need to live the life God has called me to. Although I may face many uphill journeys along the way, I know that I will finish the race, walking step-by-step with the Spirit.

BE TENACIOUS

I have traveled to Korea to minister and have had the opportunity to attend the world's largest church there. What impresses me most about my Korean sisters is their dedication to pray tenaciously until they see God move. At one event I found out that many of my Korean sisters had been up all night praying before the opening session. Though they had had no sleep, they were energized by God's answers to their prayers.

The Torch Center towers 60 stories above Seoul. Shaped like praying hands, it is home to numerous ministries and businesses, including the Korean Center for World Mission. Since the center's completion in 1991, it has become the training center for missions for a multitude of denominations across Korea. Sixty students each year receive their doctorate in missions under scholarships sponsored by the center. In 1995, 186 nations met at the Torch Center for a global congress on world evangelism. The tower is a beacon of hope to all Korea and a monument to the faith of a tiny Korean woman named Lee Hyung-Ja.

How could a tiny woman in Asia facilitate such a dramatic tower of faith and business, especially considering she was on the brink of bankruptcy just years before? The secret might be found in the basement of the Torch Center where shoes line the walls outside the prayer room. Here, prayers are offered daily in the dozens of prayer cells that run like arteries to the heart of the Korean Center for World Mission...and the heart of Lee's businesses.

Life was not always rosy for Lee. Her husband, Choi Soon-Young, had inherited the family baking business with over a million dollars in debt. They also had another family business that was draining their funds. Bankruptcy seemed inevitable. Lee was worried about her husband's health and her family's future. She rallied her strength, and in a culture where appearances and outward success are highly valued, she bowed before the bank president. The president refused her request.

Lee looked at her heart. Had she really been trusting God?

Convicted, she began to rise at 4:00 a.m. daily to pray. As she prayed, she gained confidence that God had her life and her husband's business in His hands. Soon she began to have specific answers and ideas for her husband's business. When she'd share them with her husband, he could immediately see the wisdom of these ideas. The two began to pray together every morning at 4:00. Her husband began to rely on his wife's guidance from God, calling her from work to pray over specific decisions during the day. The business began to revive, and their new construction company was building equity. Lee and her husband felt amazingly blessed, as the country of Korea was experiencing political unrest and economic downturn during this time.

> When everything around you feels as if it's falling apart and you're not sure if you can handle the fears and doubts, be tenacious and call out to God.

One morning shortly after the business began to grow, Lee was impressed by the Holy Spirit to "light every dry branch, and pass the torches from mountain peak to mountain peak. Raise the torch of the Holy Spirit high above and pass it unto the end of the world." So Lee gathered a group of four women to pray in her living room. Week after week they prayed for God's leading, their country, their families, churches, and revival. Word about the prayer meetings spread, and others joined in. Soon groups sprang up across the nation, and the decision was made to form a regular prayer meeting called the Torch Assembly.

In 1977, the Torch Assembly registered with the Ministry of Culture and Publicity as a nonprofit religious organization under its current name, the Korean Center for World Mission. In the years to follow, the idea came to build the magnificent Torch Center. And it all started with one woman's tenacious prayers and her belief that God's unlimited power would carry her family through.

PICTURING GOD IN YOUR FUTURE

Tenacity is the ability to hold on to God and allow Him to carry you through. When everything around you feels as if it's falling apart and you're not sure if you can handle the fears and doubts, be tenacious and call out to God, offer up prayer after prayer, ask for His power. And He gives it. Like Peter who walked on water in the middle of the storm, we can keep walking as long as we keep our eyes on God. The minute we rely on our own strength to see us through, however, we begin to sink.

Char Hill thinks of herself as an ordinary woman, but I know that her tenacious attitude toward life is anything but ordinary. I was introduced to Char by my sister-in-law Erin. Erin, a wonderful godly woman herself, would always tell me she wished she could have the strength and femininity of Char. Char could pour cement for a missions project in a foreign country one day, then quilt and can garden vegetables the next. She could build an entire house herself, but she also loved to nurture and mother. Erin told me that Char, who owned her own café, once held two robbers at gunpoint until the police came.

I began to see Char as some kind of modern-day pioneer woman, a Paul Bunyan of sorts, a woman of whom legends and tall tales are made! When I finally met her, however, her calm, quiet, can-do attitude was a breath of fresh air, and I began to understand where her strength comes from.[3]

"Everyone thinks I'm so strong, but they don't know my mother! I'm just a shadow of my mother," Char says.

> The things I do are normal to me. My mother was widowed three times. She had four kids when her husband had a heart attack. Pouring concrete, tearing out a tree, raising animals—this is what you had to do. If it needs done, you do it. God will take care of you, but He expects you to take care of yourself too. My mother knew God would take care of her, give her the strength no matter what, so it's natural for me to depend on God for everything.

Char grew up knowing she could achieve anything with God's help and that eternal values mattered more than pretty things or an easy life.

Char relied on the power of God to sustain her during a particularly challenging time of life:

> I had an unwanted divorce and cancer at the same time. I had two kids, both in junior high. I was alone, and I had never been alone (I married at 17). I had to let God be the man in my life. I saw my main role was to keep their lives together. God really got my attention. Physical things were not important. Who got what in the divorce was not important. I just wanted to live to raise my kids.

Char's hair grew thin. She lost weight and had blisters in her mouth and throat, so she couldn't keep food down. Things looked grim.

> I hadn't told my family I had cancer. Not wanting them to worry, I explained that I was real sick and was working hard. One day I was sitting in the back of the church, and in the middle of the sermon, the pastor stopped and said, "God wants me to pray for someone whose whole world is falling apart." Up to that point, I thought God had forgotten me. I had prayed and prayed and thought angry things like, "God, I've served You my whole life, and I am falling apart!"

Shortly after that day in church, the nurses rechecked Char's white blood cell count.

> Over and over they checked and ran tests—no cancer! It was not showing up in any of the blood work or anything. I knew then I had better stay close to God. I had better not ever get one step away from being in His will. I told God, "If You think You want me to get married again, if another man is Your will—*You* pick him out!"

Then, while helping friends move, Char met her current husband.

> He's the best thing that ever happened to me. And the doctors said I'd never have kids again—but less than a year later I was pregnant with Sarah. Looking back at disastrous things, you see they made you stronger, and I believe those things made my kids stronger. They've learned they need to give it to God, and He'll handle it.

Char had learned that life is hard. But she had also learned that the verse her mother had always quoted was true as well: "All things are possible with God" (Mark 10:27).

PICTURING GOD

When we go through rough times in life, God doesn't stand idly by. He is willing, ready, and able to intercede to accomplish His will, His perfect will. He has the power to win over anything and anyone at anytime. At times it may seem that God has abandoned us, but we can't see all the pieces of His puzzle. We lack information, perspective, and most of all, patience. But when we go to His Word and study His character, we find that God has carefully woven many pictures of Himself into the text, so we can gain a better view of who He is and how He works.

> We can't see all the pieces of God's puzzle. We lack information, perspective, and most of all, patience.

One summer I discovered many of these word pictures when I was teaching my sons about how the Bible came to us. As we followed the Bible from its initial writing to the modern translations we have today, we studied the different time periods throughout history. One day I decided to give the boys a real medieval experience by making each of them a suit of armor, a milk-carton helmet, swords, and shields. I wondered what shields were like in Bible times, and so I did some research.

I discovered that a variety of shield shapes and sizes were used during biblical times, but one type (used mostly in sieges) was a long, full-length shield. Learning this, I gained a fuller understanding of what the psalmist might have meant when he said that God was his shield. I was comforted knowing that the only way to get hurt in battle was to step out from behind the shield—or run in retreat. I also realized that because God is my shield, everything that comes to me in life must first go through Him.

God stands between me and the tsunami of responsibility threatening my world.

Intrigued, I wondered what other word pictures in the Psalms could give me insight into God's character. I discovered that God is my rock, a high place upon which a fortified city is built. I also read He is my fortress, a walled-in city. And God says He is a rampart, an elevated rise on which walls of shelter were erected in times of battle.

Now those are some word pictures I can depend on! God wants to be my high place of refuge, a place in which I can run and be safe and still have my basic needs met. He will protect me in times of battle, and I can run to Him to gain perspective on the people and things attacking my life.

Choosing to Follow the Lord

When I am tempted to give up, to throw in the towel, or to pull up short, I review the character and names of God. My favorite name of God is Jehovah-Jireh, which means "the LORD will provide." When things get tough, this name reminds me that God is my provision, and I need to choose to please Him first. During really intense times, I review a few principles:

- I will make choices based upon what will guard my integrity before God, regardless of popular opinion.

- I will ask God to go before me, to pave the way on my behalf.

- I will see if God is leading me to readjust my timing or my plan.

- I will regroup, readjust, and redelegate.

- I will rely on God's strength. I remind myself that God doesn't set me up for failure. My failures are just footsteps into the future God has for me.

I also call to mind 2 Corinthians 4:8-9: "We are hard pressed on every side, but not crushed; perplexed, but not in despair; persecuted, but not abandoned; struck down, but not destroyed." *Hard pressed* means "in a vise"—the walls are closing in. But God says we *won't* be crushed. God stands between me and the tsunami of responsibility threatening my world. Instead of worrying, instead of fuming, instead of taking my feelings out on someone else, I review God's amazing traits, sometimes out loud—because I need to hear them!

God is awesome, beautiful, caring, and compassionate. His power is unlimited, ever available, unwavering, steadfast, sure, and tenacious.

Women who have this view of God can achieve much more than those who believe in only their own power. Self-power is limited, fragile, or can be misdirected. But if we ask, God will answer, and He will send His ultimate best our way. He will provide us with the endurance we need to achieve the dreams He has given us.

Caleb and Joshua in the Old Testament provide a compelling picture of patience. Following the exodus from Egypt, Moses sent twelve men to explore the land of Canaan, but only two of them came back with the opinion that Israel should go in and possess the land God had promised them—only two were brave enough to take God at His word: Caleb and Joshua. When the rest of the nation refused to follow their lead, God banished the nation to wander in the wilderness; they would not be allowed to enter the land. But God promised Caleb and Joshua that one day they would step into the Land of Promise. That day finally arrived 40 years later.

When you wait faithfully for God, He often gives you an amazing glimpse of Himself as payment for doing the right thing day after mundane day.

Faithfulness had its payoff for Joshua and Caleb. As the first step in conquering the Promised Land, God commanded the nation to march several times around the city of Jericho, and then blow trumpets and shout. The wall of the city would collapse and give Israel its first conquest in the land. Generals of history might have had doubts about the battle plan, but not these faithful warriors. They marched, they blew the trumpets and shouted, the wall crumbled, and they began to possess the land.

Each of you will be tempted to give up (I know I've been tempted to throw in the towel a time or two hundred!). Your fears or discouragements might make you vulnerable to not believe God as you march out your God-given adventure. Keep walking. Your "Jericho Moment" is ahead.

Sarah kept walking her adventure. Raised in Alaska, she decided to serve others in her high school by being the president of her Fellowship of Christian Athletes huddle. She married and wanted to serve her community of Wasilla, so she ran for mayor and won. For most mothers, this would have been enough. But Sarah was concerned about the corruption she saw in the leadership of her home state, so she ran for lieutenant governor and lost. Undeterred, she ran for governor—and won!

Her character test came in an unexpected way. Already a mom of four, she found out she was pregnant and that the baby she carried had Down syndrome. She had always run on a prolife ticket. Would she now do what 90 percent of moms carrying a Down syndrome child do and abort this baby? No, that was not an option. Sarah decided to love and welcome this baby into the Palin family.

While dealing with her personal motherhood issue, she discovered her unmarried teenage daughter was pregnant. Would she do what many parents of pregnant teens do—whisk her away and abort her own grandchild? No, abortion was not an option. She and her brave daughter faced down the harsh scrutiny of the press and decided to welcome this new child into the Palin family.

Then her Jericho Moment came. Presidential candidate John McCain, a decorated war hero, asked Sarah to be his running mate for the White House. Sarah became the first woman vice presidential candidate for the Republican Party.

The Bible says, "Let us not become weary in doing good, for at the proper time we will reap a harvest if we do not give up" (Galatians 6:9). Your Jericho Moment is coming. Keep faithfully marching out God's adventure for your life, day after day, and one day you will see God reveal your Jericho Moment. And in your heart you will sense, "For this I was born."

𝒲INNING WORDS

When you feel tired, discouraged, and ready to throw in the towel, pray these verses over your life and dream:

> [God] sits enthroned above the circle of the earth. He stretches out the heavens like a canopy, and spreads them out like a tent to live in. He brings princes to naught and reduces the rulers of this world to nothing. "To whom will you compare me? Or who is my equal?" says the Holy One. Do you not know? Have you not heard? The LORD is the everlasting God, the Creator of the ends of the earth. He will not grow tired or weary, and his understanding no one can fathom. He gives strength to the weary and increases the power of the weak. Even youths grow tired and weary, and young men stumble and fall; but those who hope in the LORD will renew their strength. They will soar on wings like eagles; they will run and not grow weary, they will walk and not be faint.

WINNING WISDOM

Do you have a plan to handle bad days? If I have a series of strenuous, unpleasant days ahead, I begin with prayer and ask God to pull me through them. I also reward myself for getting through tough times with a favorite activity, such as calling a friend or going to the beach. Knowing there is a light at the end of the tunnel gives me the tenacity to pull through and keeps me from spiraling down into a long-term depression.

Create your own crisis plan for handling the blues—one that builds into your life and helps you deepen your walk with God. Here are a few ideas to stimulate your thinking:

- Build pictures of God into your mind by purchasing a CD of praise music or Scripture set to music. When you're having one of those days, close your eyes, put on your headset, and let His presence wash over you.

- Buy a piece of art for your office or bedroom that helps you remember your favorite attribute of God.

- Create a piece of art, screensaver, or craft to help you picture God as your strength on those bluest of days.

- Create your own retreat, someplace you can go: a quiet corner of the office, a special chair with a basket of books, a refreshing outdoor spot near a fountain or waterfall in your yard or on the patio. Open up the Psalms and gain a clear glimpse of God.

- Place something small in your wallet, checkbook, or briefcase that will remind you of an attribute of God that gives you strength—perhaps a small stone to remind you that God is your rock.

- If you have many blue days strung together, professional help may be the best plan. In every other arena of life, women of confidence go to the best when they need answers. Handling depression should be the same. Providing for your emotional health is a wise investment of God's resources.

WINNING WAYS

Do you feel as if you're running out of steam, that you cannot endure any longer? Ask God to lift you up and give you renewed energy. God will send you what and who you need to hold on to the adventure He has planned for you.

I remember a time when I was struggling with self-doubt, and I wanted to give up being an adventurer. I was feeling like a failure even though I had just experienced some of my life's greatest successes months before. I had some successful books, I was enjoying traveling for speaking and media, I had a great marriage, my three sons were all doing well, and our women's ministry had just finished a big event that had an incredible impact in our community. But I had put on some weight, I was dead-dog tired, and I needed a vacation. The straw that broke this adventurer's back was an unsigned letter of criticism I received in the mail. (I have since learned that if someone doesn't value her words enough to sign them, I will not value her words enough to read them, so in the trash it goes.) The letter was unkind, insensitive, and hurtful.

Normally I am very optimistic, but even the evidence of success in my life was being clouded over and crowded out by a growing sense of impending failure and doom. My mind was making mountains out of molehills on every front. I was thinking, *If this is the repayment for all the hard work of living out God's adventure, I want off this ride. I will just quit the adventure. This stinks, God. I want out!*

Bill had taken the boys camping, and I felt very alone and vulnerable. So I called my fine-tuning friend Debe to pray with me. She had once shared with me in one of our "fine-tuning friend meetings" that she wanted to quit her adventure, quit her family, and just run away from it all—but she couldn't figure out where to run to! I appreciated her sense of humor and candidness, so she felt safe. She had, at her moment of desperation, decided to run away to her driveway. She just sat in her car and prayed, and God sent the answer she needed.

I shared with Debe what was going on in my life, and as she prayed for me, God gave her a visual impression of what I was going through. A few days later, she sent me a card that read:

> Pam, I saw you looking into a puddle of water at your reflection. The water was so clear you could see yourself in this liquid mirror. Suddenly, someone threw a rock into the puddle. The water became rippled, and the reflection was distorted. Pam, the rock represents the person who has criticized you and hurt you, and the rippled water is how you are seeing yourself as a result. The real Pam, the one God sees, is the same one you saw in the water's reflection before the rock was thrown into the puddle. The real Pam is unharmed. *Only your image has been affected* by the rock—not the real you!

If you feel like ditching the adventure, call out to someone on your adventure team. Call out to someone who will help you cry out to God and will help you hold on to the adventure until the storm subsides.

When you see a challenge as an impossibility in your life, ask yourself if you are tackling the challenge in God's way, in His time, and with His team. Grace Cabalka saw God succeed in part because she lined up her methods with His. God calls us to function as a body (1 Corinthians 12:12-31), so Grace pulled together a quality team. God says count the costs (Luke 14:28-30), so Grace weighed out her decision carefully. God also tells us to walk in the Spirit (Galatians 5:25), so Grace asked God for His help at every step. Discuss with your fine-tuning friends or your adventure team your plan for walking out this adventure for the long haul:

- *God's order.* Are the pieces of the dream in place? Have you written a personal mission statement and a mission statement for your dream? Have you gathered resources, financing, and other practical needs to move the dream forward?

- *God's timing.* Is it time to launch the dream, push *pause* and postpone the dream, or reformat the dream? Have plans and ideas changed since you began this book? If so, how? How has God fine-tuned your dream? What changes or adjustments do you feel God wants you to make in the next few months, year, or few years to live out the dream?

- *God's team.* Who is willing to stay on your adventure team now that this study is over? Who will give you their wisdom? Their time? Their prayers? As your adventure expands, what is your plan for expanding the team? If God does through you what is beyond you, then the adventure will be too big to carry alone. How will you staff the dream as it grows?

Joni Eareckson Tada says, "Faith isn't the ability to believe long and far into the misty future. It's simply taking God at His Word and taking the next step." If you haven't stepped into God's adventure for you yet, now is the time. Step out with confidence, sister!

If you are on your adventure but discouraged, latch on to the motto on a T-shirt I bought while traveling in Oklahoma. It reads "Cowboy up!" In rodeo terms that means to ride that bucking bronco, hold on for all your worth, and ride with style until the buzzer goes off.

We women need to learn to "cowgirl up" and tenaciously ride God's adventure. So, my fellow adventurer, hang on and ride confidently and with style until you hear God say, "Well done!"

Appendix

The Names of God

*T*he more you learn about the names and attributes of God the Father, God the Son (Jesus), and God the Holy Spirit, the more your faith will grow. A few resources that have helped me grow in my view of God include: *Experiencing God* (Blackaby/King), *The Names of God* (there are several books with this title by Sumrall, Hemphill, Stone), *The Knowledge of the Holy* (Tozer), *Experiencing God's Attributes* (Myers and Myers), *God: Discovering His Character* (Bright), *Lord, I Want to Know You* (Arthur), *Your God Is Too Small* (Phillips), and *The Jesus I Never Knew* (Yancey).

Below are several names of God. When you are in a hard place, look over the list and decide what trait or name(s) of God you need to focus on, learn more about, or hang your heart and hope on. I encourage you to look up the verses and string together a few to memorize and meditate on. You can learn much by investigating a name or attribute of God. For example, when I needed God to be mighty in a situation, I gathered information from many sources to expand my view of God:

- From Lester Sumrall's *The Names of God:*

    The name "God Almighty" (or El-Shaddai in the Hebrew) emphasizes God's ability to handle any situation that confronts His people. Dr. W.A. Criswell notes that El-Shaddai "is the further enrichment of the supreme name YAHWEH. *El* is the singular form of *Elohim* and *Shaddai* is literally 'sufficient' or 'self-sufficient'; therefore, it is rendered 'almighty.' The almightiness and self-sufficiency of YAHWEH are adequate for Him to deal victoriously and even destructively with His enemies."

- From Nathan Stone's *Names of God:*

"The Almighty" in Revelation 16:7,14; 19:15 speaks of "the fierceness of the wrath of God the Almighty."

- From Phillip Yancey's *The Jesus I Never Knew:*

"The balance of power shifted more than slightly that day on Calvary because of who it was that absorbed the evil. If Jesus of Nazareth had been one more innocent victim, like King, Mandela, Havel, and Solzhenitsyn, he would have made his mark in history and faded from the scene. No religion would have sprung up around him. What changed history was the disciples' dawning awareness (it took the Resurrection to convince them) that God himself had chosen the way of weakness. The cross redefines God as One who was willing to relinquish power for the sake of love. Jesus became, in Dorothy Solle's phrase, 'God's unilateral disarmament.'

Power, no matter how well-intentioned, tends to cause suffering. Love, being vulnerable, absorbs it. In a point of convergence on a hill called Calvary, God renounced the one for the other" (pp. 204-5 emphasis mine).

- From Kay Arthur's *Lord, I Want to Know You:*

El Elyon: Most High: "For if God is not sovereign, if He is not in control, if all things are not under His dominion, then He is not the Most High, and you and I are either in the hands of fate (whatever that is), in the hands of man, or in the hands of the devil" (p. 25).

Do you see how much more I can trust God knowing that He

is completely sovereign (in control), His love absorbs all pain, His character is fierce, He is self-sufficient so He can handle any and all situations? Make it your goal to dig in and learn as much as you can about God.

NAMES OF GOD*

Advocate with the Father (1 John 2:1)

Atoning sacrifice for our sins (1 John 2:2)

Author and finisher of our faith (Hebrews 12:2)

Bread of life (John 6:35)

Bridegroom (Matthew 9:15)

Chief cornerstone (Matthew 21:42; Mark 12:10; Ephesians 2:20; 1 Peter 2:6)

Chosen of God (Luke 23:35)

Christ (Luke 9:20; 23:35; Philippians 3:8; Matthew 16:16)

Comforter (2 Corinthians 1:4)

Counselor, Wonderful (Isaiah 9:6)

Creator (Isaiah 40:28; 43:15; 1 Peter 4:19; Ecclesiastes 12:1)

Deliverer (2 Samuel 22:2; Psalm 18:2; Romans 11:26)

Door (John 10:7,9)

Dwelling place, our (Psalm 90:1)

Faithful and True (Deuteronomy 7:9; Revelation 19:11)

Father of glory (Ephesians 1:17)

Father of mercies (2 Corinthians 1:3)

Father to the fatherless (Psalm 68:5)

Father (Isaiah 9:6; 64:8; John 8:54; 17:11; 20:17; Deuteronomy 32:6)

Firstborn over all creation (Colossians 1:15)

Fortress, my (Psalm 18:2; 91:2)

Friend of tax collectors and sinners (Matthew 11:19)

God of hosts (El Sabaoth) (Psalm 80:7)

God of my salvation (Psalm 18:46)

---

* Adapted from *Experiencing God* by Henry Blackaby and Claude King (Nashville, TN: Broadman and Holman, 1994).

God and Savior Jesus Christ, our (2 Peter 1:1)

God Most High (Genesis 14:18)

God my Maker (Job 35:10)

God my Rock (Psalm 42:9)

God of Abraham, Isaac, and Jacob (Exodus 3:16)

God of all comfort (2 Corinthians 1:3)

God of all grace (1 Peter 5:10)

God of all the kingdoms of the earth (2 Kings 19:15)

God of glory (Psalm 29:3)

God of gods (Deuteronomy 10:17)

God of heaven (Genesis 24:3; Psalm 136:26)

God of the living (Matthew 22:32)

God of mercy (Psalm 59:10)

God of my salvation (Psalm 51:14; 88:1)

God of peace (Romans 16:20; 1 Thessalonians 5:23)

God of truth (Psalm 31:5; Deuteronomy 32:4)

God of the whole earth (Isaiah 54:5)

God our Father (Ephesians 1:2)

God our Savior (Jude 25)

God our strength (Psalm 81:1)

God the King of all the earth (Psalm 47:7)

God who alone is wise (1 Timothy 1:17)

God who avenges (Psalm 18:47; 94:1)

God who delivers me from my enemies (Psalm 18:47-48)

God who does wonders (Psalm 77:14)

God who forgives (Psalm 99:8)

God who hears prayer (Psalm 65:2)

God who sees (Genesis 16:13)

God, a jealous (Deuteronomy 4:24)

God Almighty (El Shaddai) (Genesis 17:1)

God, great and awesome (Daniel 9:4)

God, living and true (1 Thessalonians 1:9)

God, merciful and gracious (Exodus 34:6)

God, the everlasting (Genesis 21:33; Isaiah 40:28)

Guide, our (Psalm 48:14)

He who blots out your transgressions (Isaiah 43:25)

He who comforts you (Isaiah 51:12)

He who is able to present you faultless (Jude 24)

He who is from the beginning (1 John 2:13)

He who is ready to judge the living and the dead (1 Peter 4:5)

He who lives forever (Daniel 12:7; Revelation 10:6)

He who loves us and washed us from our sins (Revelation 1:5-6)

He who reveals His thoughts to mortals (Amos 4:13)

He who raised Christ from the dead (Romans 8:11)

He who reveals secrets (Daniel 2:29)

He who sanctifies (Hebrews 2:11)

He who searches the mind and heart (Romans 8:27; Revelation 2:23)

He who sits on the throne (Revelation 5:13)

He who was dead and came to life (Revelation 2:8)

Head (Ephesians 4:15; 5:23; Colossians 2:19)

Heir of all things (Hebrews 1:2)

Help (Psalm 27:9; 40:17; 46:1)

Helper of the fatherless (Psalm 10:14)

Hiding place, my (Psalm 32:7)

High Priest forever (Hebrews 6:20)

High Priest, great (Hebrews 4:14)

Holy One (Psalm 71:22; Isaiah 41:14; 43:15; Hosea 11:12; Luke 4:34; Acts 3:14; 1 John 2:20)

Holy Spirit (Psalm 51:11; John 14:26; Ephesians 4:30)

Hope, my (Psalm 71:5)

Husband (Hosea 2:16; Isaiah 54:5)

I AM (Exodus 3:14; John 8:58)

Image of the invisible God (Colossians 1:15)

Immanuel (God with us) (Matthew 1:23)

Immortal (1 Timothy 1:17)

Intercessor (Isaiah 53:12)

Invisible (1 Timothy 1:17)

Jealous (Exodus 34:14)

Jesus Christ our Savior (Titus 3:6)

Judge (Genesis 18:25; Judges 11:27; Psalm 7:11; 94:2; Isaiah 33:22; Acts 10:42; 2 Timothy 4:8)

Just and mighty One (Job 34:17)

King of kings (Revelation 19:16; 1 Timothy 6:15)

King of the Jews (Revelation 15:3; Matthew 27:11; John 18:39; 19:9)

Lamb of God (John 1:29; 1 Peter 1:19; Revelation 5:6-12)

Life (John 14:6; Colossians 3:4; 1 John 5:20)

Light (Isaiah 9:2; 42:6; 60:19; John 1:4-9; 8:12; Luke 2:32; 1 John 1:5)

Lord (Adonai) (Psalm 54:4)

Lord (YHWH) (Genesis 15:6)

Lord and Savior (2 Peter 3:2)

Lord God Almighty (Revelation 15:3)

Lord Is Peace (Jehovah Shalom) (Judges 6:24)

Lord Most High (Psalm 7:17)

Lord my Rock (Psalm 28:1)

Lord of the dead and the living (Romans 14:9)

Lord of glory (1 Corinthians 2:8; James 2:1)

Lord of heaven and earth (Matthew 11:25)

LORD of LORDS (Revelation 19:16)

Lord of peace (2 Thessalonians 3:16)

Lord our Maker (Psalm 95:6)

Lord Our Righteous Savior (Jeremiah 23:6; 33:16)

Lord our shield (Psalm 59:11)

Lord who heals you (Exodus 15:26)

Lord who sanctifies you (Exodus 31:13)

Lord Will Provide (Genesis 22:14)

Love (1 John 4:8)

Majesty on high (Hebrews 1:3)

Maker (Job 32:22; Psalm 95:6; Proverbs 14:31; Isaiah 54:5)

Man Jesus Christ, the (1 Timothy 2:5)

Man of sorrows (Isaiah 53:3)

Master (Luke 5:5; 2 Timothy 2:21)

Mediator of a new covenant (Hebrews 9:15)

Messiah (John 1:41)

Most Holy (Daniel 9:24)

Only Son from the Father (John 1:14)

One greater than Solomon (Matthew 12:42)

One who is and who was (Revelation 16:5)

One you are to fear (Isaiah 8:13)

Peace, our (Ephesians 2:14)

Physician (Luke 4:23)

Potter (Isaiah 64:8; Romans 9:21)

Power of God (1 Corinthians 1:24)

Prophet (Matthew 21:11; John 6:14; 7:40)

Ransom for all (1 Timothy 2:6)

Redeemer (Job 19:25; Psalm 19:14; 78:35; Proverbs 23:11; Isaiah
    47:4; 63:16)

Refiner and purifier (Malachi 3:3)

Refuge (Psalm 9:9; 28:8; 46:1,7; Isaiah 25:4; 91:2; Jeremiah 16:19;
    17:17)

Resurrection and the life (John 11:25)

Rock (Deuteronomy 32:4,15; 2 Samuel 23:3; Psalm 62:7; 95:1;
    1 Corinthians 10:4)

Ruler, blessed and only (1 Timothy 6:15)

Ruler over the kings of the earth (Revelation 1:5)

Salvation, my (Exodus 15:2; Psalm 27:1)

Savior (2 Samuel 22:3; Isaiah 43:3; 63:8; Jeremiah 14:8; Acts
    13:23; 1 Timothy 4:10; Ephesians 5:23; John 4:42)

Servant (Isaiah 53:11; Matthew 12:18; Acts 4:27)

Shelter for His people (Joel 3:16)

Shepherd (Psalm 80:1; Ecclesiastes 12:11; John 10:11; Hebrews
    13:20; 1 Peter 2:25; 5:4)

Shield (Psalm 3:3; 18:2; 28:7; 33:20)

Son of David (Matthew 1:1; Luke 20:41)

Son of Man (Matthew 12:40; 24:27)
Son of the Most High God (Mark 5:7)
Son, My beloved (Mark 1:11)
Spirit of adoption (Romans 8:15)
Spirit of glory (1 Peter 4:14)
Spirit of God (Genesis 1:2; Matthew 3:16)
Spirit of grace (Hebrews 10:29)
Spirit of holiness (Romans 1:4)
Spirit of justice (Isaiah 28:6)
Spirit of life (Romans 8:2)
Spirit of truth (John 14:17; 15:26)
Spirit of wisdom and revelation (Ephesians 1:17)
Spirit who bears witness (1 John 5:6)
Spirit who dwells in us (James 4:5)
Spirit, a new (Ezekiel 11:19; 18:31)
Spirit, eternal (Hebrews 9:14)
Spring of living water (Jeremiah 2:13)
Strength to the poor (Isaiah 25:4)
Strength, my (Psalm 28:7; 73:26; 118:14)
Stronghold (Psalm 18:2; 43:2)
Teacher (Matthew 26:18; Mark 9:17; John 3:2)
Tower, strong (Psalm 61:3)
Truth, the (John 14:6)
Vine/Vinedresser (John 15:1,5)
Way, the (John 14:6)
Wisdom of God (1 Corinthians 1:24)
Word of life (1 John 1:1)
Word (logos) (John 1:1)

Notes

Chapter 1—Speak of the Adventure: Stepping Confidently...or Not

1. J.B. Phillips, *Your God Is Too Small* (New York: Collier, 1961), 42.
2. Beth Moore, *A Taste of Believing God* (Nashville: Lifeway, 2008), 10, 13.
3. Anne Graham Lotz, ed., *Daily Light on the Daily Path* (Nashville: J. Countryman, 1998), March 8 evening reading.

Chapter 2—Stride to the Dream: The First Few Steps

1. Heather's story and quotes can be found in her book, *Listening with My Heart* (New York: Doubleday, 1997).
2. Charles R. Swindoll, *Two Steps Forward, Three Steps Back* (Nashville: Thomas Nelson Publishers, 1980), 74.
3. Thomas Edison, www.brainyquote.com/quotes/quotes/t/thomasaed104931.html.

Chapter 3—Risk: Face Down Failure

1. http://www.wisdomquotes.com/cat_failure.html.
2. The following quotes are from a personal interview with Debra Maffett on April 28, 2000.
3. Ramona Cramer Tucker, "Enough Is Enough," *Today's Christian Woman*, September–October 1996, 128.

Chapter 4—Protect the Adventure: A Winning Team

1. Martin Luther King Jr, "I Have a Dream," http://www.usconstitution.net/dream.html.
2. Richard Stengal, "Mandela, His Eight Lessons of Leadership," *Time*, July 21, 2008, 44.
3. W. Bingham Hunter, *The God Who Hears* (Downers Grove, IL: InterVarsity Press, 1986), 18.
4. Ibid., 20, 26.
5. Bill Bright, *God: Discover His Character* (Orlando, FL: New Life Publishers, 1999), 131.
6. Nathan Stone, *The Names of God* (Chicago: Moody Press, 1944), 97, 99.
7. From a personal e-mail interview with Maria and Lindsay Goff, June 2008.
8. http://www.cyc-net.org/cyc-online/cycol-0707-amato.html.
9. http://www.econ.ucsb.edu/~olivier/BD_JHR_2005.pdf.
10. http://sbinfocanada.about.com/cs/womeninbusiness/a/bizwomen.htm; http://www0.gsb.columbia.edu/null?exclusive=filemgr.download&file_id=48123&rt contentdisposition=filename%3Dkfstudy.pdf.
11. http://www.publicschoolreview.com/articles/12.
12. Inspired by Lettie Kirkpatrick, "Giving Thanks," *Christian Parenting Today*, November–December 1999 (www.christianitytoday.com/cpt/9g6/9g6054.html).

Chapter 5—Networking: The Synergy of Teamwork

1. Mary Crowley's story and quotes can be found in her book, *You Can Too* (Grand

Rapids, MI: Baker Books, 1976); Mary Kay's story and quotes can be found in her book, *Mary Kay* (New York: HarperCollins, 1994).

2. Personal e-mail to me from E. Dixon Murrah.
3. I started an organization called Seasoned Sisters (www.seasonedsisters.com) to encourage, equip, and educate women 40-65+ as we travel through this second half of life together.
4. Most of these quotes were gleaned from www.heartquotes.net/teamwork-quotes .html.
5. Crowley, *You Can Too*, 36.

Chapter 6—Energize the Adventure: It's a Mind Game

1. J.P. Moreland, *Love Your God with All Your Mind* (Colorado Springs: NavPress, 1997), 189.
2. Strong's online: http://bible.crosswalk.com/Lexicons/Hebrew/heb.cgi ?number=07965&version=kjv.
3. Monique shared her story with me in a personal interview in November 2001. Used with permission.
4. Richard A. Serrano and Amy Wallace, "San Diego Killings Make Bitter Divorce Final," *Los Angeles Times*, November 7, 1989.
5. Personal story e-mailed to me April 2006. Used with permission.

Chapter 7—Managing Your Creativity: It's All About Energy

1. Thanks to Dawn Wilson for this model of Luke 2:52.
2. www.bio-medicine.org/medicine-news/Americans-Growing-Out-Of -Shape-6447-1/.
3. www.msnbc.msn.com/id/6909463/.
4. www.ric.edu/faculty/dblanchette/ExerciseArticle.htm.
5. In the following books I explain in more detail ways to handle hard relationship obstacles: *Got Teens?* (coauthored with Jill Savage); *10 Best Decisions a Couple Can Make; 10 Best Decisions a Parent Can Make; Love, Honor and Forgive* (all coauthored with my husband, Bill).
6. www.sojournertruth.org/Library/Speeches/AintIAWoman.htm.
7. Harriet Beecher Stowe, *Sojourner Truth, The Libyan Sibyl*, posted on AFRO-American Almanac, www.toptags.com/aama/books/book6.html.
8. Ibid.

Chapter 8—Forge Forward: The Adventure in Focus

1. Helen's story and quotes can be found in her book, *The Story Goes On* (Kansas City, MO: Stonecroft Ministries, 1984).
2. www.aliveministries.net.
3. Dallas Willard, *Hearing God* (Downers Grove, IL: InterVarsity Press, 1999), 71.
4. Ibid.

Chapter 9—Endurance: She Who Hangs in the Longest Wins

1. Grace Cabalka shared her story with me through a written account she calls *Beyond Human Power*.
2. For a fuller treatment of this concept, see J.I. Packer's *Keep in Step with the Spirit* (Grand Rapids, MI: Baker Books, 2005).
3. The following quotes from Char Hill are from my personal interview with her.

For more resources to enhance your relationships and build marriages or to connect with Bill and Pam Farrel for a speaking engagement, contact

Farrel Communications
Masterful Living Ministries
3755 Avocado Boulevard, #414
La Mesa, CA 91941
800-810-4449

info@farrelcommunications.com
www.masterfulliving.com

To be a woman who maximizes midlife and beyond:
www.seasonedsisters.com

Share your adventure!
Get tips for launching your adventure
especially for readers of *Woman of Confidence*.
Register your hopes, dreams, and plans at

www.farrelcommunications.com/adventure

If you would like a list of the verses used
for Winning Words in this book, please go to
www.farrelcommunications.com/adventure

THE 10 BEST DECISIONS A WOMAN CAN MAKE
Pam Farrel

Pam encourages you to exchange the fleeting standards of the world for the steadfast truths found in a growing, fruitful relationship with God. You'll discover the joy of finding your place in God's plan as you

- realize how precious you are to the Lord
- find a positive place to direct your creativity, energy, and enthusiasm
- gain confidence regarding the value of your time and efforts

Pam's warm, motivating message will touch your heart as you seek all God has for you.

MEN ARE LIKE WAFFLES— WOMEN ARE LIKE SPAGHETTI
Bill and Pam Farrel

Bill and Pam explain why a man is like a waffle (each element of his life is in a separate box), why a woman is like spaghetti (everything in her life touches everything else), and what these differences mean. Then they show readers how to achieve more satisfying relationships. Biblical insights, sound research, humorous anecdotes, and real-life stories make this guide entertaining and practical. Readers will feast on enticing insights that include:

- letting gender differences work for them
- achieving fulfillment in romantic relationships
- coordinating parenting so kids receive good, consistent care

Much of the material in this rewarding book will also improve interactions with family, friends, and coworkers.